## Praise for *Bandwidth R*

"Although other researchers have explored the debilitating effects of racism and poverty on college students' ability to succeed, Cia Verschelden's novel perspective invigorates this discussion by uniquely employing the technological analogy of bandwidth, to make the multiple consequences of cognitive deprivation more vividly understandable than other analyses of these issues. She then infuses her book with numerous practical interventions—from neurobics mental exercises to using Pecha Kucha in the classroom—that readers can use to enhance cognitive ability and academic aptitude of their own students."—*Michael J. Cuyjet, EdD, Professor Emeritus, University of Louisville*

"Verschelden effectively immerses readers in and thereby sensitizes them to the array of economic; social; and physical, mental, and emotional realities that persistently drain nonmajority and socially marginalized students' cognitive capacities to learn. Most important, she teaches us how to recover their capacities to become successful students. . . . *Bandwidth Recovery* is a timely, essential, and uplifting read for faculty and other contributors to student learning, assisting them in drawing out those students' potential for success."—*Peggy L. Maki, education consultant specializing in assessing student learning*

"Verschelden convincingly makes the case that many lower income and minority students struggle in college not because of lower ability or poor preparation, but because they deal with life situations that deplete cognitive resources that are needed for learning. Offering us a distinctly different lens through which to view these students, she describes concrete strategies we can implement to replenish their cognitive resources so that they don't only survive, but thrive in the college environment with recovered 'bandwidth.'"—*Saundra McGuire, (ret.) Assistant Vice Chancellor and Professor of Chemistry; Director Emerita, Center for Academic Success, Louisiana State University; Author of* Teach Students How to Learn

"*Bandwidth Recovery* provides a roadmap for reversing the current trend, whereby only one in two high school students from low-income families enrolls in college in the first place, and the completion rate for those at the lowest socioeconomic rungs continues to lag far behind that of their wealthier peers. By drawing attention to the persistent economic and cultural barriers that continue to thwart the equity imperative upon which the American dream is built, Verschelden brings us closer to being able to fulfill the true promise of American higher education—that of educating for democracy."—*Lynn Pasquerella, President of the Association of American Colleges & Universities*

"*Bandwidth Recovery* is a well-written, insightful, must-read book that offers educators and counselors who work with socially marginalized youth functional strategies for promoting a growth mind-set and self-efficacy to increase learning capacity in and out of the classroom."—*Joseph L. White, PhD, Professor Emeritus of Psychology and Psychiatry, School of Social Sciences, University of California, Irvine*

BANDWIDTH RECOVERY

# BANDWIDTH RECOVERY

## Helping Students Reclaim Cognitive Resources Lost to Poverty, Racism, and Social Marginalization

*Cia Verschelden*

Foreword by

Lynn Pasquerella

Published in association with

Association
of American
Colleges and
Universities

STERLING, VIRGINIA

Published by Stylus Publishing, LLC.
22883 Quicksilver Drive
Sterling, Virginia 20166-2102

**Library of Congress Cataloging-in-Publication Data**
Names: Verschelden, Cia, 1955- author.
Title: Bandwidth recovery : helping students reclaim cognitive
resources lost to poverty, racism, and social marginalization /
Cia Verschelden ; foreword by Lynn Pasquerella.
Description: First edition. | Sterling, Virginia : Stylus Publishing,
2017. | Includes bibliographical references and index.
Identifiers: LCCN 2017007920 (print) |
LCCN 2017033905 (ebook) |
ISBN 9781620366066 (Library networkable e-edition) |
ISBN 9781620366073 (Consumer e-edition) |
ISBN 9781620366042 (cloth : alk. paper) |
ISBN 9781620366059 (pbk. : alk. paper)
Subjects: LCSH: Children with social disabilities--Education--
United States. | Students with social disabilities--United States. |
Cognition in children--Social aspects--United States. |
Education--Social aspects--United States.
Classification: LCC LC4091 (ebook) |
LCC LC4091 .V47 2017 (print) |
DDC 371.826/94--dc23
LC record available at https://lccn.loc.gov/2017007920

13-digit ISBN: 978-1-62036-604-2 (cloth)
13-digit ISBN: 978-1-62036-605-9 (paperback)
13-digit ISBN: 978-1-62036-606-6 (library networkable e-edition)
13-digit ISBN: 978-1-62036-607-3 (consumer e-edition)

Bulk Purchases

Quantity discounts are available for use in workshops and for
staff development.
Call 1-800-232-0223

First Edition, 2017

10   9   8   7   6   5   4   3   2   1

*For Patty, Emma, Abe, and John, my first children, who inspire me in this work, hoping it will contribute to the realization of a more equitable and peaceful world.*

# CONTENTS

# FOREWORD

When J. D. Vance's (2016) best-selling memoir *Hillbilly Elegy: A Memoir of a Family and Culture in Crisis* took the literary world by storm just prior to the 2016 presidential election, it served as a stark reminder to leaders in higher education of the extent to which increasing access to educational opportunities alone is not sufficient to destabilize the reproduction of social inequality in the academy. Vance exemplified Chicago School sociologist Robert Ezra Park's concept of the *marginal man*, which he defined as "one whom fate has condemned to live in two societies and in two, not merely different but antagonistic cultures" (Park, 1928, p. 892). Park's description of the marginal man's conflict of the divided self as resulting from the "life and traditions of two distinct peoples; never quite willing to break, even if he were permitted to do so, with his past and his traditions, and not quite accepted . . . in the new society in which he now sought to find a place" (Park, 1928, p. 892) is developed and enhanced by Cia Verschelden. In her compelling and groundbreaking analysis of how factors such as poverty, racism, and social marginalization contribute to diminished cognitive resources, she unveils how the human tendency to arrive at group identities around race, class, gender, and culture serves to perpetuate a growing economic segregation in higher education.

For those like Vance, who occupy an interstitial space, there is equal familiarity with two cultures without the feeling of being at home in either. The data confirm what we already know: There is a psychic toll exacted on the poor, on first-generation college students, and on individuals from underrepresented groups that results from a lack of social and cultural capital, along with the absence of social networks and a sense of belonging. What we have paid less attention to in academia are the real costs associated with achieving upward mobility, often involving cultural fears and political resentments. Although Vance described both the social awkwardness of attending lavish parties at his Ivy League alma mater and the discomfort of knowing that he would be viewed by many at home as "getting too big for his britches" (Vance, 2016, p. 30), he also revealed the stigma of socioeconomic ascent he felt from the other side. Thus, he confessed, "It's not just our own communities that reinforce the outsider attitude. It's the places and people that upward mobility connects us with" (p. 206).

However, the lost cognitive resources to which Verschelden points are not merely a consequence of feeling like an outsider. In their March 2017 report of the Wisconsin HOPE Lab, Sarah Goldrick-Rab, Jed Richardson, and Anthony Hernandez highlighted growing rates of food insecurity among community college students, with two out of three students experiencing this phenomenon. At the same time, the authors noted that half of students in community colleges are facing shelter insecurities, and 13% to 14% identify as homeless. It should come as no surprise, then, that under such circumstances, students have reduced cognitive resources and mental bandwidth, diminishing the likelihood of their learning, persisting, and graduating from college.

Nevertheless, Verschelden rejects a deficit perspective, which focuses on what students are missing, and instead offers evidence-based interventions and strategies for recovering mental bandwidth and promoting student success. Through the targeting of cognitive, noncognitive, and psychosocial factors, she demonstrates how we can create learning environments that help students reclaim some of these cognitive resources and reach their full potential.

*Bandwidth Recovery: Helping Students Reclaim Cognitive Resources Lost to Poverty, Racism, and Social Marginalization* provides a road map for reversing the current trend, whereby only one in two high school students from low-income families enrolls in college in the first place, and the completion rate for those at the lowest socioeconomic rungs continues to lag far behind that of their wealthier peers. By drawing attention to the persistent economic and cultural barriers that continue to thwart the equity imperative on which the American dream is built, Verschelden brings us closer to being able to fulfill the true promise of American higher education—that of educating for democracy.

In reflecting on Verschelden's call to action and the collective work ahead of us, I was reminded of a book of poetry I came upon a few years ago, written by Emma Willard, the legendary champion of education for girls and women. As it turns out, the volume was titled *The Fulfillment of a Promise* (1831). Though her poems were never the subject of great literary acclaim, there is a singular image in one of her works that comes to mind when I think about the leadership role higher education must play in promoting social mobility, justice, and equity for all. In the poem, Willard described her sister, Anna, who had just recovered from a period of lengthy illness. The couplet reads, "And never had we known how sweet this scene / When Anna's self in Anna's form is seen."

I love the line "When Anna's self in Anna's form is seen." It speaks of transformation, in this case recovery from illness. But it also illuminates what

Verschelden is enjoining us to do—to educate students so that their selves can emerge, and they can live the full potential of their life to see their world beyond the front door, find their passions, align the person they are with the person they hope to be, and help each and every student find their selves in their forms.

Lynn Pasquerella
President
Association of American Colleges & Universities

## References

Goldrick-Rab, S., Richardson, J., & Hernandez, A. (2017). *Hungry and homeless in college: Results from a national study of basic needs insecurity in higher education.* Madison, WI: Wisconsin HOPE Lab and Association of Community College Trustees.

Park, R. E. (1928). Human migration and the marginal man. *American Journal of Sociology, 33*(6), 881–893.

Vance, J. D. (2016). *Hillbilly elegy: A memoir of a family and culture in crisis.* New York, NY: Harper.

Willard, E. (1831). *The fulfillment of a promise; by which poems, by Emma Willard are published, and affectionately inscribed to her past and present pupils.* New York, NY: White, Gallaher, & White.

### References

Du「uring the summer and fall of 2016, we witnessed a presidential campaign season that, in my life, has no match for its negativity and its
focus on fear, hate, and division. In my view, at the heart of much of
the angst is the outrageous—and still growing—degree of economic inequality in the United States. Millions of people feel completely left out of the
political and economic process, and the now virtually mythical "American
dream" is out of reach for most people at the bottom of the status hierarchy.
In this environment, it's no wonder that people's base instincts for survival
and for protecting their own at the expense of "others" had great appeal. It
is at times like these that it is imperative that higher education, once known
as "the great leveler," again be that beacon of hope for otherwise disenfran-
chised people.

As was evident in campaign rhetoric, there seems to be significant lack
of agreement on so many major social issues, from the environment to public education to the economy. The one thing we can all agree on is that we
have some serious challenges ahead; we need to focus the best of our minds
and intellects on finding solutions. It is completely unacceptable that we
are squandering the brainpower of over half our young people because of
the negative effects of racism, poverty, and social marginalization, such as
happens to members of nonmajority racial and ethnic groups, people who
are considered different based on affectional orientation or gender identity,
people who live with chronic economic insecurity, and others about whom
there are negative stereotypes.[1]

I will provide evidence that members of these groups systematically
experience conditions in their life, based on one or more of these identities,
that result in chronic stress and, therefore, decreased physical and mental
health and social and economic opportunity. The cost of the many kinds
of scarcity in their life—money, health, respect, safety, affirmation, choices,
belonging—is seriously reduced "mental bandwidth" (Mullainathan &
Shafir, 2013). *Bandwidth* refers to the cognitive and emotional resources
needed to deal with making good decisions, learning, caring for family, having healthy relationships, and more. People who are operating with depleted
mental bandwidth can face serious challenges in achieving academic success, starting in childhood (Levy, Heissel, Richeson, & Adam, 2016), and

are much less likely to make it to college. For those who do make it, their bandwidth capacity often keeps them from learning and, therefore, persisting and graduating from college.

A variety of interventions have been tried in high schools and colleges that have shown some promise for helping students gain back bandwidth. I will provide information on these evidence-based strategies and share some other ideas based on my work and the work of many colleagues who are valiantly trying to help students succeed in college against significant odds. These interventions are for inside and outside the classroom and address not only cognitive processes but also sociopsychological, noncognitive factors that are relevant to the college environment as a whole. This book will be helpful, therefore, to instructors, student affairs professionals, and college and university administrators, all of whom have an interest in creating learning environments where all students have a chance to succeed.

We absolutely need fundamental change in U.S. society so that more than half of our young people are not at educational and life disadvantages; until that happens, however, we need to work to increase the chances of those students in our colleges and universities. I nurture the hope that if more students could get the support they need to succeed in college, they could be the change agents who work to transform our society into a place in which all children have an equal chance to fulfill their potential.

## Note on the Strengths Perspective

A social worker by training and temperament, I must address how I see the concepts in this book as coming from what the social worker profession calls a "strengths perspective." From the title, a reader might conclude that this is just another tale about why poor, nonmajority people are not or cannot be successful in college. Social workers call this a "deficit perspective," in which we focus on what students in these groups do not have and the ways in which their preparation or capabilities fall short of the mark. On the contrary, I assert that these students are as capable as any of succeeding when they have the full complement of their mental bandwidth available to them. In fact, many students who have grown up with some adversity bring with them "funds of knowledge" (see chapter 11) that contribute to their resilience and achievement orientation that other students lack entirely.

A focus on recovering mental bandwidth lost to poverty, racism, and social marginalization is, in my view, a very positive approach that acknowledges the inherent ability and amazing potential of every student. It does not blame people—not the student and not the faculty. I am not suggesting that faculty or administrators are racist, or classist, or homophobic. I am asserting that there is overwhelming evidence that, in the United States, systems of racism, social marginalization, and extreme economic inequality have devastating effects on the life of millions of people. I argue in this book that we in higher education can, by understanding these social realities, help our students recover the mental bandwidth necessary for them to reach their academic, personal, and career potential.

## Note

1. See Jiang, Ekono, and Skinner (2015) for statistics on children in poverty. See Casselman (2014) for college enrollment statistics by family income, Association of American Colleges & Universities (2015) for statistics on bachelor's degree attainment by race/ethnicity, and National KIDS COUNT (2015) for the percentage of nonmajority children who live in poverty.

# ACKNOWLEDGMENTS

Thanks to my children and my students, from whom I have learned most of what I know that matters and who inspire me to keep learning and teaching.

Thanks to Tina Bhargava for her collaborative thinking about many of the critical issues in the book. Thanks to Emma Mercier and Bill Richter who actually read the manuscript twice through and gave me excellent feedback and advice. Juanita McGowan and Chez Redmond gave me helpful insight into the experience of Black students and how to frame the book in reality and hope. David Macey and Brenton Wimmer gave me valuable counsel on chapter 9. Mary Pezza and David Lowry asked critical questions that helped clarify my thinking. Jim Watson lent me his neurobics, a concept he created when he was a faculty person in design. Rukmini Ravikumar, another design colleague, created the brains graphics. Each of your spirits lives in these pages.

Thanks in advance to all of my colleagues who will read this book and use the ideas, and expand them, to help students regain mental bandwidth so they can be more successful in academics, career, and life. And thanks to all those students who will use their educations to create a society in which books like this will be history.

# INTRODUCTION

I grew up in a very small Catholic town in Kansas, with my parents and my six siblings, above the family funeral home. A major university was 30 miles away; my aunts and uncles went there, and my older sister and brother were there when I set off for the big campus town. We didn't have scholarships, and we weren't in the honors program, if there even was one at that time. Our parents had saved money over the years, and they paid our tuition (about $1,000 a semester for however many credit hours we could manage). My siblings and I all had jobs, earning the rest of the money we needed for housing and food. I never had a car or even a bicycle. I lived in a cockroach-infested (seriously!) apartment and walked to school and work. Even considering the cockroaches, I was a privileged White student with plenty of social and cultural capital, so I could devote all my cognitive resources to learning.

Just like in the 1970s when I started at the university, the reality of higher education today is that it's not a resource equally available to all. Students in certain groups arrive at college, if they get there at all, with a diminished capacity to learn due to the negative effects of racism, poverty, and social marginalization, which have robbed them of cognitive resources for learning. Fortunately, there are ways we can create learning environments in which these students can reclaim some of those cognitive resources so they can learn and make progress toward a positive future in which they can reach their full potential.

In spite of the fact that race is only a social construct and that law and public policy agree that people should not be treated differently based on physical differences, it remains true there are serious costs to being Black, Hispanic, or Native American in the United States. Compared to the White majority, these nonmajority groups score significantly worse on nearly every quality-of-life metric, including physical and mental health, employment, housing, crime, incarceration, education, income, and wealth. They are more likely to have asthma, high blood pressure, diabetes, and heart disease (Barr, 2014). They have higher levels of unemployment (V. Wilson & Bivens, 2014) and underemployment (McMahon & Horning, 2013) and are more likely to be homeless or experience housing insecurity (da Costa Nunez, 2012; National Coalition for the Homeless, 2009). They are more likely to

1

commit crimes for which they receive disproportionately longer sentences (M. Alexander, 2012; Farbota, 2016; Federal Bureau of Prisons, 2016; Sakala, 2014). People in these groups have lower educational attainment and significantly lower incomes and personal wealth (Barr, 2014; McMahon & Horning, 2013). The experience of poverty in itself, for both majority and nonmajority people, reduces cognitive resources (Mullainathan & Shafir, 2013), resulting in a tremendous waste of human potential.

When students have been raised in conditions of economic insecurity and/or are members of a nonmajority group[1] and have lived with discrimination and exclusion for their entire life, they are most likely functioning with limited cognitive resources for learning and success in college. There are many programs that help these students get into college and remedial classes to help them catch up academically, but the results are discouraging in terms of retention and graduation rates. Income is a very significant factor for entering college; high school graduates from high-income families go to college at a rate of 82%, compared to 52% for those from low-income families (Casselman, 2014). For college graduation, race/ethnicity is the more important predictor. Of people in the United States 25 years old and older, 51% of Asians, 35% of Whites, 21% of Blacks, 17% of American Indians/ Alaska Natives, and 15% of Hispanics have a bachelor's degree or higher (Association of American Colleges & Universities, 2015). Black males, at the statistical bottom of the college success data, have a six-year graduation rate of only 34% compared with 48% for all students (U.S. Department of Education, 2010, in Harper & Kuykendall, 2012).

In spite of well-designed and well-intentioned engagement and support strategies for nonmajority and economically insecure students, the data remain discouraging. We have made it financially possible for students to enroll in college, and we have provided academic and social interventions to help them, and with that done, they are expected to get on with school and to succeed just like majority students who didn't grow up experiencing racism and/or economic insecurity. Our practice suggests that these students are no different from other students in terms of cognitive resources; all they need is a bit of a boost, and they should be able to find their way. In this book, I assert that these students *are* qualitatively different from majority students who come from backgrounds of relative social and economic security. They are very likely operating with only a small fraction of their cognitive resources available for learning, given their other responsibilities and concerns related to work, family, community, and mere survival in the face of a lifetime of being Black (or Hispanic or Native American); poor; lesbian, gay, bisexual, or transgender (LGBT); or a member of another nonmajority group in the United States.

# Note

1. *Nonmajority* includes people who are lesbian, gay, bisexual, or transgender (LGBT), many of whom have grown up facing homophobia and heterosexism. They suffer the ill effects of persistent stress and the resultant loss of bandwidth for learning in college. Their experience is the focus of chapter 9.

# PART ONE

## THE COSTS OF RACISM, POVERTY, AND SOCIAL MARGINALIZATION

*Like a lot of white people, I had envisioned racism as a series of distinct, objectionable, even violent acts . . . and had not really grasped that it was also, perhaps primarily, a relentless, wearying drone of negativity from which there is no escape.*

—Christina Thompson (2008, p. 193)

I f it's obvious to you from your knowledge or your lived experience that being poor or existing in a social environment thick with negativity and disrespect leaves a person short on available cognitive resources, then skip to Part Two. Part One of this book is meant to make the case that persistent worry about money, including lack of regular access to adequate food, shelter, health care, safety, and so on, takes up parts of the brain that are then not available for thinking, learning, and making good choices. In addition, members of certain racial or ethnic groups in the United States—for instance, Black, Hispanic, and Native American, and some other minority groups—on their worst days exist within a dusty cloud of fear, worry, isolation, and frustration that robs them of available cognitive resources.

Although many people will still deny it, and more of us wish it were not true, there is ample evidence that racism and poverty make people sick, waste human capital, and diminish cognitive resources. There are many reasons that some of us, maybe especially those of us who have a relatively privileged life, would rather not face up to the facts. Perhaps most important and discomfiting to acknowledge is that the systems of discrimination, hostility, and inequality that are the manifestations of racism and unfettered capitalism

seem to have benefited us at the expense of others. In addition, it is particularly disturbing, if one faces facts, that we could do something about these
phenomena if there were the political and popular will to do so. Thus, we
have a situation in which we live in one of the wealthiest and most resource-
rich countries in the world, and yet we allow social and economic conditions
to strangle the potential of well over half our citizens. It is an upsetting realization, and it is no surprise that most of us, especially those of us who are not
subject to such deprivations, would rather not think about it.

The costs of racism and poverty cannot be denied. When I talk about
racism, I am referring not only to subtle and very unsubtle discrimination,
hostility, and violence but also to the "relentless, wearying drone of negativity" (C. Thompson, 2008) that is the reality of life in the United States for
many Blacks, Hispanics, Native Americans, and other people who do not fit
into someone's idea of the mainstream. Camara Jones (2016), the president
of the American Public Health Association, defined *racism* as

> a system of structuring opportunity and assigning value based on race . . .
> the social interpretation of how we look that unfairly disadvantages some
> individuals and communities, unfairly advantages other individuals and
> communities, and saps the strength of the whole society through the waste
> of human resources.

In the documentary series *Unnatural Causes . . . Is Inequality Making Us Sick?*
(California Newsreel, 2008), physicians and social scientists painted a sober-
ing picture of the health costs of racism and poverty. In the United States,
health and wealth are in nearly perfect alignment; poor people are sicker, and
rich people are healthier. Nonmajority people are sicker than majority people,
even taking into account income and wealth. Beyond the economic realities
of paying for both preventative and time-of-illness health care, what other
factors can explain these health disparities? The researchers concluded that
racism and poverty make people sick (California Newsreel, 2008).

In addition, there are sociopsychological phenomena that result in serious impairment in mind, spirit, and cognitive resources. These phenomena are about the way racial and ethnic minority people are treated. These
include microaggressions, stereotype threat, belongingness uncertainty, and
other sociopsychological *underminers,* so named because when they are
part of lived reality, they act to undermine and diminish cognitive capacity.
When people live with persistent racism, their cognitive resources are limited
because they are devoting so much psychic energy to keeping their heads up
against this constant barrage. These sociopsychological phenomena will be
the focus of Part Two.

Economic insecurity, like racism, can have a negative effect on cognitive resources, what Mullainathan and Shafir (2013) called "mental bandwidth" (p. 41). In their 2013 book *Scarcity: The New Science of Having Less and How It Defines Our Lives*, Mullainathan and Shafir demonstrated with their own research and that of many other social scientists that the condition of scarcity depletes mental capacity; in their terms, *bandwidth*. The authors told us that poverty comes with a "bandwidth tax" (p. 39). To help us understand the effects of scarcity, Mullainathan wrote about how he made mistakes when he got overcommitted, like missing deadlines and double booking meetings. He used himself as an example of how scarcity—in his case, a scarcity of time— taxed his mental bandwidth so much that it affected his work performance.

What we usually mean by the term *poverty* is people who are economically insecure, who live in a persistent condition of scarcity. Mullainathan and Shafir (2013) conducted social experiments in which they simulated a situation of scarcity by having adult participants imagine that they need to make a decision about whether to have $300 worth of repairs on their car or risk it breaking down, after which they gave the participants a short IQ test. They found no significant difference between the scores of rich people and poor people. In a follow-up study, however, the researchers raised the cost of the repairs from $300 to $3,000. Under this condition, they found that the scores of rich people were not affected, but the scores of the poor people fell the equivalent of 14 IQ points. This is a worse erosion of cognitive performance than being sleep deprived by staying awake for 24 hours before the test. The stress and the mental strain for a poor person faced with this unexpected extra cost "depletes the amount of mental bandwidth available for everything else" (Feinberg, 2015, p. 40).

We often hear that poor people make bad decisions that result in their staying poor. Poor students are less likely to go to college, and those who go are less likely to finish than wealthier students. Poor people take out loans before payday; then, when they can't pay them back on time, they end up paying ridiculous amounts of interest, making them even poorer. From the perspective that scarcity diminishes bandwidth, it's not that poor people make bad decisions as much as that the condition of being poor constrains the ability to make good decisions in an environment that promotes bad decisions. This understanding should make us take a step back when we blame our financially strapped students when they seem to *choose* not to study or come to class and appear to lack the motivation to succeed. They may be highly motivated but are just out of bandwidth because of many hours of paid work or worry over not having enough money or other resources.

And what about those students who will arrive at college over the next decade? In the United States in 2013, there were 72 million children younger than 18 years. Of those, 45% (32 million) lived in low-income families (200% of the federal poverty threshold), and half of those lived in poor families (at or below the *federal poverty threshold*, defined as $23,624 for a family of four in 2013); both groups of children are being raised in conditions of persistent scarcity (Jiang, Ekono, & Skinner, 2015). Children growing up in economically insecure families have a difficult time succeeding at school and in other areas of their life. They are, like their parents, operating with diminished bandwidth for learning and for making good choices, resulting in low rates of high school completion, college attendance, persistence, and graduation. In the United States, lifetime outcomes for college graduates are so much more positive in terms of health, wealth, and economic and intellectual contribution that we can no longer afford to have well over half of the population left out of the opportunity.

In regard to the negative health outcomes of chronic stress, information from the documentary *Unnatural Causes . . . Is Inequality Making Us Sick?* (California Newsreel, 2008, "Chronic Stress," para. 7) tells us the following:

> People who are lower on the socioeconomic pyramid tend to be exposed to more formidable and ongoing stressors, e.g., job insecurity, unpaid bills, inadequate childcare, underperforming schools, and dangerous or toxic living conditions, crowded homes, even noisy streets. They are also less likely to have access to the money, power, status, knowledge, social connections and other resources they need to gain control over these many tempests that threaten to upset their lives. (Chronic Stress, para. 7)

Racism and poverty rob people of mental bandwidth, leaving them with limited cognitive resources to learn and perform to their potential and resulting in the national tragedy of blighted hope and squandered human capacity for creativity and problem-solving.

# I

---

# PHYSICAL HEALTH

In explaining the phenomenon of the bandwidth tax, Mullainathan and Shafir (2013) referred to *"tunneling,* [a term] meant to evoke tunnel vision, the narrowing of the visual field in which objects inside the tunnel come into sharper focus while rendering us blind to everything peripheral, outside the tunnel" (p. 29). When a person is sick or has a sick child or parent, she will tunnel on that sickness. If the person is also poor, the tunneling is not only about the illness itself but also about all the costs in money, time, and other resources that are necessary to deal with treatments, transportation, special school or living accommodations, and so on. With at least part of her mind continually focused on the worry and logistics of dealing with ill health, she has limited cognitive resources to devote to anything else. This is how ill health steals bandwidth.

Many of us have short periods when we are not feeling well. We might have seasonal allergies, or we catch a flu bug from an office mate, or we injure our back playing football with the neighborhood kids. For those of us with adequate financial resources and social supports, these are most often temporary inconveniences, and we weather them well, confident that in a few days we'll be back on our feet with no long-term harm to our personal or work life. Sometimes one of our children is sick, and we have to rearrange our schedule to make doctor visits and to care for that child at home. Some of us have parents with health problems, some of them very complex and difficult, and we experience more serious disruptions. During particularly difficult times, or if our parents live far away from us, we may experience the kind of stress and worry that leaves us, temporarily, with diminished bandwidth for the rest of our responsibilities. These are the times when, if we think about it, we might be able to come close to understanding what it is like to operate day to day with less than our full mental capacity. However, for those of us who have sufficient resources, even these pressing challenges get resolved, and we are able to resume our normal life.

## Chronic Stress

People who are poor and sick have less of a chance for everything to work out well—and they know it. Living under conditions of persistent scarcity at the bottom of the social hierarchy results in the kind of stress that actually, in itself, makes people sick. In his book on health disparities in the United States, Donald Barr (2014) defined *health* as "a state of complete physical, mental and social well-being and not merely the absence of disease or infirmity. . . . Health involves health of the body, health of the mind and the emotions, and health of the social context in which one lives" (p. 14). The likelihood of a life that is mostly healthy, by this definition, is significantly decreased for people who are at the bottom end of the social strata.

The unrelenting stress of being poor can cause damage to bodies and immune systems, making people more susceptible to illness. Goode (2002) called this "the heavy cost of chronic stress."

> Prolonged or severe stress has been shown to weaken the immune system, strain the heart, damage memory cells in the brain and deposit fat at the waist rather than the hips and buttocks (a risk factor for heart disease, cancer, and other illnesses). Stress has been implicated in aging, depression, heart disease, rheumatoid arthritis and diabetes. . . . Stress may be a thread tying together many illnesses that were previously thought to be unrelated. (para. 5, 9)

Goode went on to say, "Perhaps the best indicator of how people are likely to be affected by stress is their position in the social hierarchy" (para. 41).

It is one of the functions of our brain to register danger and give us the message to act to avoid it. The hypothalamus is the part of the brain that monitors and responds to stress (McEwen, 2002). Our brain also contains an allostatic control mechanism that keeps us on an even keel and helps us cope with challenges. Our brain detects stress consciously and unconsciously. At the point that we become conscious of the threat, the conscious message is sent to the hypothalamus, but psychological sources of stress also trigger a response in the hypothalamus that might never make it to our conscious awareness. From the hypothalamus, a message is sent to the pituitary gland, the brain's message center. The pituitary gland receives messages from the brain and converts them into hormones, which are then secreted into the bloodstream, each targeting a specific part of the body and telling it to activate or not. In the case of stress, the adrenal gland is the targeted body part.

When the adrenal gland receives the stress message, it immediately sends into the bloodstream two hormones, epinephrine and norepinephrine. These cause what we think of as the "adrenaline rush" that makes our heart beat faster, our breathing deepen, and our muscles tense for flight. The adrenal gland produces another hormone, cortisol, which kicks in and turns off more slowly than adrenaline. Cortisol immediately assists epinephrine and norepinephrine and helps our body over the long term (Barr, 2014).

> This combined control mechanism involving sensing stress in the hypothalamus, sending control hormones from the pituitary that results in the release of epinephrine, norepinephrine, and cortisol from the adrenal gland, is often referred to as the hypothalamic-pituitary-adrenal axis (HPA). The level at which this allostatic control mechanism is functioning is referred to as the allostatic load. The higher the level of stress response hormones circulating in the blood, the higher the allostatic load. (Barr, 2014, p. 60)

For normal stress response, our body's allostatic load is maintained at a state of readiness. When we experience a stressful episode, the allostatic load begins to rise; plateaus at the elevated level; and when the stress is over, it slowly returns to its original state. Afterward, our body recharges the adrenal gland so it has sufficient supplies of the stress hormones to be ready for the next stressful period.

If, however, stress is continuous or nearly so, the body has no chance to fully recharge, and it has a chronically elevated allostatic load. This elevated load results in higher than normal amounts of the stress hormones circulating in the bloodstream, causing the inflammation of cells through the release of certain chemicals, affecting the way blood flows through the body. Inflammation can cause injury to the cells; such injury can lead to thickening and stiffening of the arteries. This condition is "highly predictive of future cardiovascular disease such as heart attack and stroke" (Barr, 2014, p. 63). The Framingham Heart Study, which has been tracking heart disease in community-based cohorts for more than 50 years, found an inverse relationship between socioeconomic position and the biomarkers for heart disease (Loucks et al., 2010). And the effects start early and last a lifetime:

> Repeated activation of the stress response early in life can literally affect the wiring of the brain, inhibit children's ability to develop "resilience," and increase the chances they will develop helplessness, anger and depression later in life and become more susceptible to obesity and illness. (California Newsreel, 2008)

Persistent stress results in a chronically elevated allostatic load, which contributes to increased incidence of disease. What factors explain the relationship between having a low position in the social hierarchy and stress? Living in economic poverty, a state in which people are perpetually short of the money required for the most basic needs like food and shelter, is itself a powerful stressor. In the United States, a society in which many people still deny the existence of a stratified class system, the reality is that economic poverty equals low social status. In practical terms, that means people experience a scarcity of respect, voice, access to power, and a sense of being an equal player in their community. This scarcity can be defined as *social capital*, which "refers to the collective value of all 'social networks' [who people know] and the inclinations that arise from these networks to do things for each other ['norms of reciprocity']" (Harvard Kennedy School, n.d., para. 1). Of course, within the larger sense of the U.S. "community," there are communities in neighborhoods, for instance, in which even the most economically insecure people experience positive relationships of mutual support. From a political power perspective, however, people who lack social capital are left out of the larger community and live their life outside many public and private systems of mutual benefit. They have very little voice in community decisions and operate outside of the informal and formal political processes. As Wilkinson (1999) said about increasing economic inequality,

> As social status differences in a society increase, the quality of social relations deteriorate. . . . Health and the quality of social relations in a society vary inversely with how hierarchical the social hierarchy is. (pp. 50–51)

People who are left out suffer the negative health effects caused by chronic stress, whereas those who have social capital actually gain health. For instance, from a study of the power of social ties to increase immunity to the common cold, S. Cohen, Doyle, Skoner, Rabin, and Gwaltney (1997) found that people with three or fewer types of social relationships (e.g., family, friends, fellow workers, or church members) were four times more likely to get a virus-induced cold than those who reported having six or more types. The greater the inequality in a society, the worse the negative effects on the people at the bottom of the hierarchy. In the United States, economic inequality has been on the rise since 1980 (Stone, Trisi, Sherman, & Horton, 2016). Wilkerson (1999) reminded us that as perceived levels of inequality change, so does the nature of social relations. People's perception of their connection to, or alienation from, their community is an expression of social capital that is, in turn, associated with allostatic load, which helps some handle stresses and makes others much more likely to have serious chronic health challenges.

People who live in low socioeconomic status (SES) conditions live in neighborhoods that have low social capital. They "experience both more environmentally related illness and additional stress related to the characteristics of their neighborhoods" (Barr, 2014, p. 135). Some aspects of low social capital include violence, hostility, social anxiety, and increased perception of discrimination.

> The constant stress created by living under these conditions will lead to chronically elevated levels of stressor hormones, which over time will lead to cellular damage, illness, and ultimately to premature death. One's perceptions of his or her connection to, or alienation from, the surrounding community creates a form or social capital, which in turn is associated with allostatic load. (Barr, 2014, p. 75)

Being poor can stress us out. Being stressed out can make us sick. In addition, the United States is a country in which there is a high correlation between race and income/wealth. What happens if a person is poor *and* a member of a nonmajority group? Before going any further with a focus on *race*, I want to be clear that I realize that *race* is a social construct and that there are no significant differences among people based on their skin color or their facial characteristics. However, I will use the term because it is a tremendously powerful and dug-in social construct in the United States that is used to maintain systems of power and privilege. We can say, truthfully, that "there is no such thing as race," but for nonmajority people in the United States, this thing that doesn't exist is very real every moment of their life. So, I will use the term *race* to distinguish the major groups in the United States—White, Black, Asian, Native American—and sometimes *race/ethnicity* to acknowledge major ethnic identities, such as Hispanic. Of course, we know that *White* is not a race, but we use the term to describe people of European descent.

## Correlates of Health

As groups in the United States, Blacks, Hispanics, and Native Americans have consistently worse health outcomes than Whites. Because there are no significant inherent biological (genetic) differences among these groups, what could explain this persistent pattern? According to Barr (2014), part of the explanation is in the data on the SES of people in these racial/ethnic groups. In this country, "educational attainment is a principle measure of SES, and is strongly associated with other measures of SES, such as income, and with health status" (Barr, 2014, p. 118). As is summarized in Table 1.1, people in nonmajority groups attain much lower educational levels than do White people.

Income data show gross disparities among full-time, year-round workers. In 2014, the median annual income for all U.S. households was $53,657. For White households, median income was $60,256, whereas the equivalent income for Black households was $35,398 and $42,491 for Hispanic households (DeNavas-Walt & Proctor, 2015). Barr (2014) reminded us that a high percentage of Black and Hispanic workers are unemployed or employed part-time, so these disparate figures for median household income understate the real differences. The problem is exacerbated because although educational attainment increases income for all groups, it does not increase equally. At every level of education, from less than high school to a master's degree, Black and Hispanic workers earn significantly lower salaries than their White counterparts with the same level of education (Barr, 2014).

It is clear that both poverty and low educational attainment are highly correlated with poor health outcomes and that race is intimately intertwined with both of those factors in the United States. But even if we control for income and education, does simply being a member of a nonmajority group contribute to ill health? There is growing evidence that it does. In the following section on health inequities, we will focus on the Black population, as it has, in general, the worst health outcomes of any group. However,

TABLE 1.1
**Educational Attainment by Race and Ethnicity in the United States**

|  | All (%) | White (%) | Black (%) | Hispanic (%) | Native American (%) |
|---|---|---|---|---|---|
| Less than high school | 6.5[a] | 5.2[a] | 7.4[a] | 10.6[a] | 22.0[b] |
| High school or higher | 91.2 | 95.4 | 92.5 | 77.1 | 86.7 |
| Bachelor's degree or higher | 35.6 | 43.0 | 21.3 | 16.4 | 15.3 |
| Master's degree or higher | 8.7 | 10.1 | 5.0 | 3.2 | No data |

*Note.* From "Percentage of Persons 25 to 29 Years Old With Selected Levels of Educational Attainment, by Race/Ethnicity and Sex: Selected Years, 1920 Through 2015," by Digest of Education Statistics, 2015b, https://nces.ed.gov/programs/digest/d13/tables/dt13_104.20.asp
a. From "Percentage of High School Dropouts Among Persons 16 to 24 Years Old (Status Dropout Rate), by Sex and Race/Ethnicity: Selected Years 1960 Through 2014," by Digest of Education Statistics, 2015a, https://nces.ed.gov/programs/digest/d15/tables/dt15_219.70.asp
b. From "2010–2012 American Community Survey 3-Year Estimates, U.S. Census Bureau, U.S. Department of Commerce (Nov. 14, 2013)," in *2014 Native Youth Report* by Executive Office of the President, December 2014, Washington, DC, The White House.

presumably all poor people, people of color, and those in other nonmajority groups experience the negative effects of poverty and racism in proportion to their level of economic deprivation and the negative stereotyping of their group.

One indicator of the degree of ill health among Black people is the concentration of Blacks in a neighborhood or area. In general, the higher the concentration, the lower the health status of Black people. A study in Massachusetts showed that health disparities by neighborhood persisted even after taking into account SES, the negative effects of poor neighborhoods being more serious for Blacks than for Whites (Subramanian, Chen, Rehkopf, Waterman, & Krieger, 2005). LeClere, Rogers, and Peters (1997) found a high correlation between the concentration of Blacks in neighborhoods and higher death rates. The higher the percentage of Blacks in the neighborhood, the higher the death rate, at all SES levels, but especially in low-income neighborhoods. Other studies on health indicators have provided evidence that people are less healthy in neighborhoods with high concentrations of Black people, demonstrated by, for example, lower rates of survival to age 70 years (Cullen, Cummins, & Fuchs, 2012) and higher rates of breast cancer deaths (Whitman, Orsi, & Hurlbert, 2012), low-birth-weight infants (Debbink & Bader, 2011), and lung cancer deaths (Hayanga, Zeliadt, & Backhus, 2011). D. Phuong Do (2009) found that persistent neighborhood poverty, rather than individual SES, was highly correlated with adverse health outcomes and confirmed that Blacks were disproportionately exposed to this type of long-term poverty. She concluded,

> Chronic exposure to poor neighborhoods by blacks helps explain the black/white health disparity. . . . The enduring effects of segregation and neighborhood poverty in perpetuating racial health disparities become even more salient when we consider the strong likelihood for black families of residing in impoverished neighborhoods across successive generations. (p. 1374)

These data illustrate institutional racism in systematic neglect—a breakdown of the social contract—in these neighborhoods. Two other negative health indicators that seem to implicate racism as the primary factor are birth outcomes for Black mothers and the heightened risk of illness and premature death for Black people who successfully escape their disadvantaged upbringing.

## Birth Outcomes

Black women disproportionately give birth to preterm and low-birth-weight infants, and a greater percentage of Black infants die in their first year than infants in other groups. These statistics hold true even when we control for household income and level of education. These indicators, along with life expectancy, serve as important expressions of overall population health. Many researchers have tried to explain this phenomenon of disproportionately negative birth outcomes for U.S.-born Black women. Researchers at the University of Illinois at Chicago (2007) concluded, "The cause of low birth weights among African-American women has more to do with racism than with race." Virtually every study has come to the same conclusion.

Black women give birth to preterm (before 37 weeks gestation) infants at double the rate of White women. An infant is considered low birth weight (LBW) if he or she weighs less than 2,500 grams (5.5 pounds) and very low birth weight (VLBW) if he or she weighs less than 1,500 grams (3.25 pounds). In 2013, 8% of infants born in the United States were born at LBW and 1.4% at VLBW. For infants of Black mothers, the rates were 12.8% and 2.8%, respectively, and for White mothers the rates were 7% and 1.1%, respectively (Martin, Hamilton, Osterman, Curtin, & Matthews, 2015). In 2013, Black infants were twice as likely as White infants to die in the first year of life (Matthews, MacDorman, & Thoma, 2015).

There is a strong association between preterm birth and both birth weight and death in the first year of life (Matthews et al., 2015). The reasons that Black mothers are more likely to give birth to preterm, LBW infants are not precisely clear, but there is growing evidence that it has to do with the way that elevated levels of stress hormones affect "fetal programming." The fetal programming hypothesis "suggests that stimuli during critical periods of embryonic and fetal development may alter such development and influence lifelong health" (Molnar, 2015, para. 9).

There have been many studies of birth outcomes for Black women that have looked at the issue from a variety of perspectives. Some focus on the fact that the higher the number of self-reported incidents of personally experienced racism, the higher the likelihood that a woman has elevated levels of stress hormones (Collins, David, Handler, Wall, & Andes, 2004; Dominguez, 2008; Giscombé & Lobel, 2005), even after controlling for medical and sociodemographic risk factors (Dominguez, Dunkel-Schetter, Glynn, Hobel, & Sandman, 2008). Elevated levels of these hormones, in turn, are associated with preterm births (Makrigiannakis et al., 2007; Rich-Edwards & Grizzard, 2005; L. Rosenberg, Palmer, Wise, Horton, & Corwin, 2002; Sandman et al., 2006; Wadhwa et al., 2004) and LBW and VLBW infants (Collins et al., 2004). For Black mothers, knowing that their children will also experience racism comes with a stress cost in itself (Nuru-Jeter et al., 2009). Braveman (2008) described this as "pervasive vigilance" (PowerPoint slide 21), referring to a Black mother who constantly anticipates threats to herself or her children. Ertel and colleagues (2012) identified the correlation between racism and depression in pregnant Black women of low SES and the association of depression with preterm and LBW infants. Barnes (2008) learned from study participants that "the experience of stress and racism are constant factors in African-American women's lives and are inseparable from their pregnancy experiences" (p. 293).

The path toward adverse birth outcomes for Black women starts when they are infants and young girls. A life of racism causes wear and tear on people's bodies, in what some people refer to as *weathering*, and contributes to racial health disparities. Weathering is a result of persistently elevated allostatic load, which is highest among Black women (compared to both White women and Black men), possibly due to the double discrimination of racism and sexism (Geronimus, Hicken, Keene, & Bound, 2006). Of course, any condition of ill health can contribute to negative birth outcomes for pregnant women. The inflammation caused by stress can negatively affect birth outcomes (Christian, Glaser, Porter, & Iams, 2013). Then, during pregnancy, cortisol can cross the placental barrier and affect fetal development and have lifelong health consequences for the child (Challis, 2004; de Weerth & Buitelaar, 2005; Kuzawa & Sweet, 2009). Tollenaar, Beijers, Jansen, Riksen-Walraven, and de Weerth (2011) identified three potential pathways for stress to cause changes in fetal programming: Cortisol could cross the blood–brain barrier to affect brain development in the fetus; stress may constrict blood flow to the fetus, decreasing available nutrients and oxygen; and stress might cause changes in the mother's behavior, such as eating patterns or increased tobacco and alcohol consumption. And the pattern starts over with the new child.

Why the emphasis on birth outcomes when I am talking about the mental bandwidth of college students to learn and have academic success? I use this research to illustrate the strength of racism to do real physical harm, even negatively affecting Black children in the womb. Women in their reproductive years are amazingly resilient, which explains the continuation of the human species. Women are built to carry, give birth to, and feed and nurture their offspring. The fact that the psychophysiological force of racism is so strong as to threaten the very life of Black infants and potentially have deleterious effects on their health as adults tells us that the likelihood that racism can rob our students of critical mental bandwidth is extremely high. Add to that the stress of our Black students who are also parents and have the distraction of knowing that their children are experiencing racism and that they are often helpless to protect them.

## John Henryism and "Skin-Deep" Resilience

In addition to the threat to reproductive women and their children, weathering affects Black women and men, especially those who buck the system, who actually persist and succeed in spite of the battering effects of racism. In what Hamblin (2015) called "the paradox of effort," Black people who use tremendous resources of self-control and determination to get out of the environment of their poor upbringing get rewarded with accelerated aging and higher rates of hypertension and heart disease. This phenomenon was called "John Henryism" by Sherman James (1994), who recalled the story of John Henry. In the late 1800s, Henry reputedly beat a steam-driven drill in a race to drive in a railroad spike and died from the effort. James referred to "high effort" coping, which he described as "sustained cognitive and emotional engagement" (p. 165), like the kind that nonmajority people must use every day. James suggested that John Henryism began among Black people following the Civil War as a cultural adaptation as they began to construct for themselves an "*American* identity."

> To be authentic that identity had to, first of all, acknowledge and find meaning in their past enslavement. Second, it had to make possible a culturally coherent (for Blacks themselves) expression of core American values such as "hard work," "self-reliance," and "freedom." And, finally, it had to provide a pragmatic (i.e., peaceful and effective) means to resist the new forms of oppression to which they, even as "freed" people, were being increasingly subjected. With its strong, explicit emphasis on hard work and self-reliance, and its equally strong but more implicit emphasis on resistance to environmental forces that arbitrarily constrain personal freedom, the concept of "*John Henryism*" embodies, albeit imperfectly, all of the above. (pp. 178–179)

The costs of resiliency and self-control start early. Young people who, through their own self-control and resiliency, defy the odds and come to college from childhoods of poverty, poor schools, and unsafe neighborhoods may have health challenges. In their study of nearly 300 Black youth aged 17 to 20 years, G. E. Miller, Yu, Chen, and Brody (2015) found, "Despite academic success and healthy lifestyles, these youth showed relatively poor cardiometabolic health at age 20 years, as reflected in obesity, blood pressure, and stress hormones" (p. 10326). The outward success of these young people makes it look like they have transformed their lives in a positive way and may mask underlying health problems, in what the researchers referred to as "skin-deep" resiliency (p. 10326).

When we meet these young people as college students, it is easy to conclude that they have overcome their disadvantaged pasts, but that is only partially true. They are operating with bandwidth taxes from racism and poverty, and they well may have ongoing health concerns that are robbing even more of their attentional resources. The kind of self-control that our students must use every day can trigger the persistent release of stress hormones, with rare opportunities for breaks to recharge, which contributes to ill health. We need to recognize that what looks like coping may be only "skin deep," and we need to work on ways to help our students continue without the high costs to current and future health.

# 2

# MENTAL HEALTH

The concept of resiliency leads us to think about the effects of racism and poverty on mental health. According to the U.S. Public Health Service,

> Mental health is fundamental to overall health and productivity. It is the basis for successful contributions to family, community, and society. Throughout the lifespan, mental health is the wellspring of thinking and communication skills. (Department of Health and Human Services, n.d., p. 1)

The fact that *mental illness*, by definition, uses up mental bandwidth seems self-evident. In addition, mental illness correlates strongly with many chronic physical diseases such as cardiovascular disease, diabetes, obesity, asthma, epilepsy, and cancer (Centers for Disease Control and Prevention [CDC], n.d.). People with a mental illness are less likely to get adequate medical care and stick with treatment plans for their chronic diseases and are more likely to use tobacco and abuse alcohol (Centers for Disease Control and Prevention, n.d.).

People living in poverty are more likely to have a mental illness than people who are more financially secure. Growing up poor increases a person's likelihood of having a mental illness (Gilman, Kawachi, Fitzmaurice, & Buka, 2003), and, as found in a longitudinal study of Native American children, moving out of poverty decreases mental illness to the level found in families that had never been poor (Costello, Compton, Keeler, & Anglold, 2003). Sometimes we think that the mental illness caused the poverty, but "poverty, acting through economic stressors such as unemployment and lack of affordable housing, is more likely to precede mental illness than the reverse" (Florida Council for Community Mental Health, 2007, p. 1). And "socioeconomic status shapes a person's exposure to psychosocial, environmental, behavioral, and biomedical risk factors that directly and indirectly affect mental health" (Centers for Disease Control and Prevention, 2004, in Florida Council for Community Mental Health, 2007). Helping people out of poverty can have positive effects on mental health. Entin (2011) found, "As economic status improved, the clinical symptoms continued to improve, which created a 'virtuous cycle of increasing returns'" (para. 6).

Compared to 10% of children in the general population, 21% of children in low-income families have a mental health problem; 57% of these children live in families at or below the federal poverty threshold. The large majority of children, 75% to 80%, according to the National Center for Children in Poverty, who need mental health services don't get them (Masi & Cooper, 2006). It is clear that our students who grew up poor might bring mental health challenges to college with them, where the challenges will continue to rob the students of bandwidth.

According to the World Health Organization (2007), the "best evidence indicates that the relationship between mental ill-health and poverty is cyclical: poverty increases the risk of mental disorders and having a mental disorder increases the likelihood of descending into poverty" (p. 1). Manderscheid (2013) asserted,

> Those who are poor are subjected to physical and sexual abuse, psychological trauma, fear and danger, unhealthy lifestyles and neighborhoods, and the personal consequences of high-risk behaviors . . . less accessible healthcare. . . . Mental illness entraps people in poverty. Not only does it rob one of the vision, motivation, and drive needed to move out of poverty, but it also leads to debilitating social isolation, so that one is not even aware of opportunities when they infrequently do arise. (para. 4, 6)

How do Blacks and other minority groups fare, when we take out the specific effects of poverty, on the question of mental illness? Interestingly, there seems to be some contradiction in the data. Although most studies show that mental illness is correlated with racial minority status, McGuire and Miranda (2008) stated, "Minorities have, in general, equal or better mental health than white Americans, yet they suffer from disparities in mental health care" (p. 393). Four studies conducted by the National Institute of Mental Health, found that Black, Hispanic, and Asian groups (with the exception of Puerto Ricans) "reported lower rates of lifetime mental disorders than white Americans reported" (McGuire & Miranda, 2008). Most other sources suggest that people in minority groups suffer more mental illness than Whites and all agree that these groups, Blacks especially, underutilize mental health services. Blacks and Hispanics use about half of the outpatient mental health services (counseling or medication) that Whites use (Substance Abuse and Mental Health Services Administration, 2015). Much of this disparity can be attributed to structural barriers, such as lack of transportation, insufficient numbers of care providers, cost of care, and lack of or inadequate insurance (Substance Abuse and Mental Health Services Administration, 2015).

In addition to structural barriers, why might mental illness be under-reported and undertreated in minority communities? Samantha Irby (2015) in an essay about her own path to mental health treatment recounted the following:

> When I finally got help for my mental illness, I was sure I was letting Rosa Parks and Harriet Tubman down by talking about my silly little feelings (subtitle). . . . No one in my house was talking about depression. That's something that happened to white people on television, not a thing that could take down a Strong Black Woman. . . . I come from the kind of people whose response to "Hey, man I'm pretty bummed out" is "Shut up, there's nothing wrong with you." (para. 2, 4)

Researchers have examined the reasons that Black people don't seek treatment for mental illness. Lack of cultural competence in diagnosis and treatment might be one explanation. Blow and colleagues (2004) found that Blacks were four times as likely to be diagnosed with schizophrenia as Whites, even though the disorder is evenly distributed among all ethnic groups. They thought that one problem was that non-Black doctors used themselves as the model, so that behavior that sounded unusual was called psychotic. They gave the example of a Black person who reported feeling paranoid and how from some people's point of view that is a healthy and rational feeling given the perceptions of Blacks in U.S. society (Blow et al., 2004). Psychiatrist Heather Hall, who works with psychiatric patients, observed,

> People say minorities don't follow up [in psychiatric care]. Maybe on their first session they are not heard. Why would they come back? If I tell a therapist I am being brutalized and he thinks I'm delusional, why would I come back? (Vedantam, 2005)

Underlying the relationship between mental illness and minority status are the historical realities of different groups: violence against and almost complete decimation of Native Americans, slavery of Blacks, the exploitation of the labor of Mexican and Chinese workers, the internment of Japanese Americans, and so on. The results of these and other historic traumas are manifest still today in the exclusion of some groups from social, educational, and economic resources that keep well-being out of reach for many.

# 3

# HUMAN CAPACITY

*We all bear the societal burden of lost productivity, increased disability, higher crime, welfare and prison costs, not to mention the human cost of thwarted hopes, dreams and health.*

—California Newsreel (2008)

Because of the negative effects of poverty and racism, millions of people in the United States are unable to access their complete brain capacity to learn and contribute to their full potential. In 2013, 39% of Black children, 37% of Native American children, and 33% of Hispanic children lived in families with incomes at or below the federal poverty threshold compared to 14% of non-Hispanic White children (National KIDS COUNT, 2015). Given the deleterious effects of poverty and racism on health and mental health, the tremendous waste of human capital is clear. How much of their mental bandwidth will these kids have when they arrive on the doorsteps of our colleges and universities?

How did things get so out of balance? One factor is wages for average American workers. Real wages for workers in the United States have been stagnant since the 1970s, whereas the incomes of the top 1% have increased 156%, and those of the top 0.1% have increased by 362%. As a result, in 2014, the bottom 20% of wage earners got only 3.6% of all income, whereas the top 20% took in nearly 50%. Even more unbalanced is wealth; the top 20% own 80% of the wealth in the United States (Powell, 2016). This imbalance happened somewhat gradually since the 1970s with a combination of deregulation of business and banks, drastic cuts in social safety net programs, and erosion in the power of labor unions. According to Lawrence Katz,

> The problem of inequality in income, wealth, and political power is exacerbated by another issue. America's vaunted economic mobility has become decidedly less so, making it increasingly likely that where you start out financially is where you'll wind up. (Powell, 2016)

23

In addition to the trillion-dollar actual cost of poverty and racism, the death of the American dream seems a huge cost in itself, the end of optimism and hope. I have not seen a study of the cost in mental bandwidth of the lack of hope, but it is surely high.

Referring to findings from the study titled "The Business Case for Racial Equity," D. Alexander (2013) stated,

> Racism has left a vast legacy of violence. Bigotry in America has marginalized a diverse range of minority cultures. It dashes the hopes of children. . . . Bias based on race costs the United States a shade under $2 trillion a year. (para. 1, 2)

A more diverse workforce in which there is increased equality is good for business. "A well-educated, healthy, and diverse workforce is essential for improving economic efficiency and competing in a global marketplace" (A. Turner, 2013). If incomes of minorities were equal to the incomes of White Americans, total earnings would increase by 12%, or $1 trillion (A. Turner, 2013, p. 6); the U.S. Department of Commerce estimates that minority purchasing power would increase from $4.3 trillion to $6.1 trillion by 2045. Closing the earning gap would increase federal tax revenue by more than $1 trillion by 2030. Even a 10% reduction in Medicaid and income support would reduce government expenditures on these programs by $100 billion. According to the Institute of Medicine, the indirect economic cost of preventable chronic disease may be more than $1 trillion per year (Harvard School of Public Health, 2012). Health inequities cost the health care system $24 billion a year (A. Turner, 2013).

There are many other areas in U.S. society where racism and discrimination have resulted in persistent inequities across race and ethnicity. Access to affordable housing and safe neighborhoods is still elusive for many minority families. Public schools have resegregated since the 1980s.

> The average white public school student attends a school that is almost 80% white. In contrast, 72% of black and 77% of Hispanic students attend schools where the majority of students are minorities. . . . Half of all black and Hispanic students attend schools where 75% of all students are poor. Only 5% of whites attend such schools. (A. Turner, 2013, p. 11)

Because most public schools in the United States are funded primarily with property tax dollars, poor students go to poor schools that have inadequate facilities, high teacher turnover, fewer electives such as art and music, and are in neighborhoods that are less safe (C. Turner et al., 2016).

In contrast, higher education has been called "the great equalizer." Is getting to college the ticket to success for students from disadvantaged neighborhoods and public schools? Not necessarily. The number of poor students going to college has increased in the past few decades, but graduation rates have declined. For students from families in the lowest income quartile, bachelor's degree attainment fell from 12% in 1970 to 10% in 2014. Fewer than 25% of students from families with incomes less than $10,000 earn bachelor's degrees, whereas the rate is 67% for those from families earning more than $150,000 (Fischer, 2016). According to Thomas G. Mortenson, "the rich are getting richer because of higher education, and the poor are getting poorer because of it" (Fischer, 2016). Anthony P. Carnevale added that higher education "takes the inequality given to it and magnifies it. It's an inequality machine" (Fischer, 2016). Of course, the answer is to significantly decrease economic inequality nationally, but until that happens, we have to figure out how to help our students recover bandwidth so they have a fighting chance to succeed academically. We can no longer afford to waste the brainpower of generations of young people.

# 4

# LOSS OF COGNITIVE RESOURCES AND BANDWIDTH

## Scarcity

A t every moment, about 11 million bits per second of processing are active in our brain. We have conscious control of fewer than 100 of them. As in Figure 4.1, just the few white connections are what we can control. (This diagram is not to scale, of course, but you get the idea.)

Our students come to college with varying amounts of mental bandwidth available for learning. As I mentioned earlier, when I went to college, I went with most of my brain ready to learn. I went to a large university 30 miles from my hometown, where my older brother and sister were also students. All of my paternal aunts and uncles had gone there as well. My parents had saved some money, so my tuition was covered. I worked 20 or so hours a week to pay for rent and other living expenses. I was a White student who received an adequate education in a Catholic elementary school and a small-town high school. I was healthy, safe, and loved. All of my mental bandwidth was intact; I had full access to all of my cognitive resources.

Many college students are not so lucky. Many grew up in economic insecurity and are still in that reality. As Mullainathan and Shafir (2013) stated, poverty robs mental bandwidth. So, many students routinely have to "spend" some of their bandwidth on working to make money as well as worrying about not having enough. Because of poverty, some of their bandwidth is now "X'ed out," no longer available for learning. In the illustration shown in Figure 4.2, the area in black is still available (again, representative, not scientific).

**Figure 4.1.** Our brain with full function.

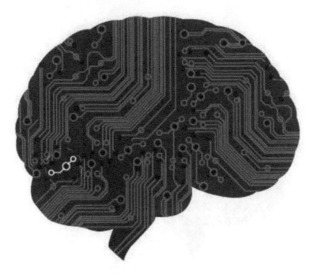

**Figure 4.2.** The poverty tax to mental bandwidth.

Now, think about what happens if those poor students are also Black; Hispanic; Native American; Asian; or gay, lesbian, or transgender. And what if they live in a city and go to a school where they experience racism or homophobia or some other "differentism" and so live in the negative soup of stereotyping and discrimination? (*Differentism* is defined as the negative attitude or behavior of a person toward another person who does not conform

**Figure 4.3.** Bandwidth lost to exclusion and hostility based on race.

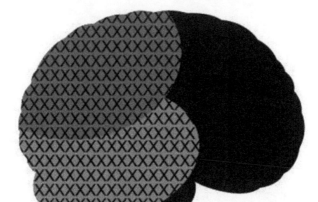

to his or her conceptualization of "normal.") Remember Mullainathan and Shafir's (2013) assertion that "scarcity robs mental bandwidth"? This is, in essence, another kind of scarcity. These students experience scarcity of respect, esteem, safety, and acceptance. In Figure 4.3, we see that even more mental bandwidth is X'ed out by the experience of social exclusion and hostility.

For Black students, we could probably cross out a bit more because they often have to maintain what W.E.B. Du Bois called *double consciousness*. Black students, because of the long history of racism in the United States, have to have two identities—their true one and another one that takes into account the way they are seen by White people—and adapt behavior accordingly. Discussing the related concept of "code-switching," which originally referred to bilingual language usage, Gene Demby stated,

> We're looking at code-switching a little more broadly: many of us subtly, reflexively change the way we express ourselves all the time. We're hop-scotching between different cultural and linguistic spaces and different parts of our own identities—sometimes within a single interaction. (R.L.G., 2013, para. 1)

It sounds exhausting! Some researchers have suggested that this pressure may contribute to mental health problems for Black students (Green, 2016). The same is true for LGBT students, which I will address specifically in chapter 9.

Students who don't have adequate financial resources or have to work too many hours are constantly preoccupied with money concerns. They worry about how they will pay their bills and, for many who have families to support, how they will keep their children (or their parents or siblings) fed and healthy. This kind of persistent worry can make you sick (American Public Health Association, 2015). Add to that the ill health that is associated with racism and we have to subtract yet more bandwidth (see Figure 4.4) because now the student must also think about and suffer from physical illness, yet another kind of scarcity, the scarcity of physical well-being.

Now we have students who, on a good day, are operating with much less than half of their brainpower. Imagine sitting in a college classroom with one ear and one eye closed and music playing so loudly that it is hard to hear the professor. No matter how hard you try, you miss out on too much and your concentration is shot. That's just a simple picture of the situation related to cognitive or attentional resources that some students experience every day.

Mullainathan and Shafir (2013) explained that there are two parts of mental bandwidth that affect our ability to learn and to make choices. The first part is *cognitive capacity*, which we usually think about as the part that we need to succeed at school and work. We need to be able to think clearly and to take in new ideas and instructions. The second part is *executive control*, which they said "underlies our ability to manage our cognitive activities, including planning, attention, initiating and inhibiting actions, and controlling impulses" (Mullainathan & Shafir, 2013, p. 47). Students whose

**Figure 4.4.** More bandwidth lost to chronic illness.

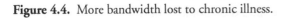

bandwidth is depleted are less able to "keep their head in the game." When they're worried and broke and feel isolated, it's difficult for them to focus on long-term goals enough to give up the video game for an hour of studying or to set an alarm and get up for that 8:00 a.m. class. This can be construed as a lack of self-control, which some people see as an aspect of personal strength or discipline, but this perspective ignores the fact that the actions that we typically call *self-control* require the use of those limited executive control resources. In other words, self-control requires bandwidth that students just don't have. Students' capacity for persistence is diminished, and school might lose out to life's other demands. Even if students somehow find the self-control to focus on academics, they may do half as well with only half of their cognitive resources available for the task. It is easy to understand why they might give up altogether.

With competing demands for attention, what these students are doing is multitasking, which we have come to think about as the ability to do several things simultaneously. However, Doyle and Zakrajsek (2013) asserted that even though we think we are doing two or more things at once, we are really switching back and forth between the separate tasks or thoughts. Each time we do that, it takes a bit of time to refocus. So when a student is in class but is worried about how she will make her paycheck last to the end of the month or is trying to figure out if a snarky comment had racist intent, she is unable, at the same time, to absorb what the teacher is saying. Even when she tries to get her focus back in the classroom, the residual lag time steals even more of her attention. Some of us might be able to identify a bit if we've had competing responsibilities like managing a career and raising small children. When we're at work, we feel like we should be home with the kids, and when we're at home, the demands at work are nagging at our attention. The result can be a sense that we're not doing either task as well as we could and should.

# PART TWO

# SOCIOPSYCHOLOGICAL
# UNDERMINERS

In Part One, I addressed the costs of poverty and racism (and other negative "isms") to physical and mental health and to human capital in general. At the foundation of much of these costs are sociopsychological phenomena that result in serious impairment in mind, spirit, and cognitive resources. These phenomena are experienced by racial and ethnic minorities; LGBT people; and others who don't fit someone's idea of normal, including women in many settings. What I term *underminers* contribute to what Christina Thompson (2008) called the "relentless, wearying drone of negativity from which there is no escape" (p. 193) and take an awful toll on bandwidth. These underminers include microaggressions, stereotype threat, disidentification with academics, and belongingness uncertainty. When people live with these underminers, their cognitive resources are diminished because they are devoting so much psychic energy to keeping their heads up against this constant toxic barrage. Green (2016) asserted,

> College campuses haven't shielded students from the effects of societal racism—and at times they have exacerbated it. . . . Many students of color not only have to battle institutional racism, they also have to engage in academic environments that condone microaggressions and stereotyping. This can make these students feel like they have to outshine their peers in the classroom to disprove the notion that they are academically inferior. (para. 8, 9)

This scarcity of basic respect and acceptance, and even safety from aggression, carries a heavy bandwidth tax. This shows up clearly in differential college outcomes for various groups.

# 5

# MICROAGGRESSIONS AND "MODERN RACISM"

One of the worst underminers is a scarcity of basic respect, affirmation, and psychological safety for students who are members of certain nonmajority groups. A manifestation of this scarcity is the social phenomenon of microaggressions. This phenomenon is part of what has been called "modern racism" (Carter, Peery, Richeson, & Murphy, 2015, p. 242) or "aversive racism" (Pearson, Dovidio, & Gaertner, 2009, p. 314). W. A. Smith, Yosso, and Solórzano (2006) called the consequence "racial battle fatigue" (p. 300). I think this phenomenon could be called the *super-underminer* that undergirds all of the others. The toll for members of non-majority groups, who live with racism (or classism or homophobia or other differentism, in general) every day, is measurable and, I suspect for most of us who are part of the majority most of the time, nearly incomprehensible.

This modern racism is a bit like air pollution; it is sometimes invisible, but you always know it is there. Many of us may have felt it at some time in our life when we were in the minority in a specific setting or when we were clearly not part of the favored group. I remember a trip to Jamaica with our children when our two Black sons were part of the majority, at home in their own skin, and the rest of us were the minority, clearly outsiders. In sports competitions in my youth, I was among the more skilled players; today my slower reflexes make me feel inadequate and unworthy to be anything more than the last picked for the team. For most of us, these are passing situations, and when they are over, we're not left drained and discouraged. The experience of everyday racism is different. It is relentless. Arienne Thompson (2014) wrote, "We are exhausted. We are tired. We can't breathe" (para. 5). One of her friends described that "being Black in America is like walking through an ice storm: It's cold, isolating, and exhausting" (para. 17). Evan Narcisse (2014) wrote about the dilemma of what to tell his young daughter about racism. Does he warn her to be vigilant, "to bob and weave and dodge it" (para. 10), or hold back and risk her coming upon it unprepared? He is past discouraged: "I also know it'd be stupid to think that things will change in my lifetime. I'm at the end of hope" (para. 12). Might our students be similarly discouraged and even hopeless when they encounter personal or institutional racism in an environment where they've come to learn and prepare themselves for a better future?

What makes modern racism so exhausting is, partially, its subtlety. Old style racism, the in-your-face kind, was at least clear. No cognitive energy was needed to recognize and process that this was a racist environment or that a particular action had racist intent. The Association for Psychological Science (2007) explained it this way:

> The problem is that we have limited cognitive resources, so when we are solving one problem, we have difficulty focusing on another at the same time. Some psychologists reason from this that subtle racism might actually be more, not less, damaging than the plain antipathy of yesterday, sapping more mental energy. (para. 4)

This is what Mullainathan and Shafir (2013) called a "bandwidth tax." According to Luczaj (2008), when racism is subtle, people can

> waste a great deal of energy trying to understand what is happening. . . . I would suggest that energy on all levels, emotional, physical and spiritual, is wasted in such unclear situations. And people in such circumstances become unable to use their full potential. (para. 4)

Derald Wing Sue (2003) agreed that this modern form of racism is "many times over more problematic, damaging, and injurious to persons of color than overt racist acts" (p. 48). Thinking about our nonmajority students who have to navigate their way through college with this added demand on their mental bandwidth, we can understand why they might not achieve to the best of their ability. "Many blacks . . . have developed coping strategies for the most hateful kinds of racism; it's the constant, vague, just-below-the-surface acts of racism that impair performance, day in and day out" (Association for Psychological Science, 2007, para. 9).

The term *microaggression* has been used to describe this subtle phenomenon, the just-below-the-surface words or acts that keep the target off balance. According to Sue and his colleagues (2007),

> Racial microaggressions are brief and commonplace daily verbal, behavioral, or environmental indignities, whether intentional or unintentional, that communicate hostile, derogatory, or negative racial slights and insults

toward people of color. Perpetrators of microaggressions are often unaware that they engage in such communications when they interact with racial/ethnic minorities. (p. 271)

I want to briefly focus on the word *daily* from Sue's quote. These are not incidents that happen once in a while or only in specific circumstances that a person could most of the time avoid. These are a part of the daily fabric of the life of people of color and others who have some "different" identity from the majority. New Zealand Aborginal writer Sam Watson said,

> It was hard . . . for people who had not experienced sustained, persistent discrimination to understand what it was like to be suspected every single day, by someone, somewhere, of having done something wrong or underhanded, of having nicked something, or lied, or broken the law. It was exhausting, he said, having to defend yourself against this barrage of suspicion. "It just wears you down after a while." (C. Thompson, 2008, p. 193)

Sue and colleagues (2007) described three forms of microaggressions: *microassault, microinsult,* and *microinvalidations,* defined as follows:

> A microassault is an explicit racial derogation characterized primarily by a verbal or nonverbal attack meant to hurt the intended victim through name-calling, avoidant behavior, or purposeful actions.
>
> A microinsult is characterized by communications that convey rudeness and insensitivity and demean a person's racial heritage or identity.
>
> Microinvalidations are characterized by communications that exclude, negate, or nullify the psychological thoughts, feelings, or experiential reality of a person of color. (p. 274)

Pierce, Carew, Pierce-Gonzales, and Willis (1978) described these acts as "subtle, stunning, often automatic" (p. 66), packing a powerful punch but just enough under the radar as to prevent anyone from confronting the deed or the doer. These behaviors or comments are so insidious precisely because they are subtle, very possibly unintended, and often perceived as trivial and not worth challenging.

Sue and his colleagues (2007) shared many examples of each of these forms of microaggression according to various themes such as "ascription of intelligence" and "myth of meritocracy" and "second-class citizen" (pp. 276–277). Our students could surely add many more to the list from their own experience. Table 5.1 lists just a few illustrations of each form.

**TABLE 5.1**

**Examples of Microaggressions Toward College Students**

| Microaggressions | Examples |
|---|---|
| Microassaults | • Saying, "You don't belong here. Go back home!"<br>• A store owner following a person of color around in the store*<br>• Barring a person from entry into an event based on his or her assumed group membership<br>• Engaging in racial profiling as law enforcement<br>• Restricting a person's freedom of movement on campus based on his or her assumed group membership |
| Microinsults | • Assuming that Black, Hispanic, and Native American students are probably not prepared for college<br>• Saying, "You are so articulate!" (to a Black student)*<br>• Saying, "You're different, not like most of your group" |
| Microinvalidations | • Saying, "You won't succeed here. This is not a place for you."<br>• Saying, "When I look at you, I don't see color."<br>• Saying, "It's easy for Blacks to get into this graduate program because they're minorities."<br>• Saying, "As a woman, I know what you go through as a racial minority."*<br>• Saying, "You're an outsider. You don't exist." |

*Note.* Asterisks denote examples from Sue and colleagues (2007, p. 276).

Not everyone thinks that the concept of microaggressions is legitimate. Some people are concerned that we're encouraging students to be whiners and be overly sensitive to slights that are not intended as such. Lukianoff and Haidt (2015) contended, in regard to microaggressions, that students would be better served if they were taught to practice a psychological strategy called "cognitive behavioral therapy," in which they reexamine, in a nonemotional way, things that have happened or that have been said. The goal is to identify distortions in thinking and, thereby, realize that no real offense was intended, so none should be felt.

Through cognitive behavior therapy, a student, for instance, can "minimize distorted thinking and see the world more accurately" (Lukianoff & Haidt, 2015, para. 18). Through this process, the student can

> describe the facts of the situation, consider alternative interpretations, and then choose an interpretation of events more in line with those facts. Your emotions follow your new interpretation. In time, this process becomes automatic. When people improve their mental hygiene in this way—

when they free themselves from the repetitive irrational thoughts that had previously filled so much of their consciousness—they become less depressed, anxious, and angry. (para. 18)

Interestingly, I teach a similar technique called "rational self-analysis" (Zastrow & Kirst-Ashman, 2013, p. 373) through which students learn a process to potentially change their self-talk (or help someone else to) concerning an event about which they have negative feelings. The first step is to do a "reality check" on the report of the event. The students try to, rationally and calmly, double-check if they've reported the circumstances how they really happened. If, for instance, someone made a veiled racist (or classist or sexist) comment, and this was confirmed by witnesses, and the person feels assaulted or insulted or invalidated by the incident, those seem like legitimate emotions to feel. This might be what Lukianoff and Haidt (2015) criticized as "emotional reasoning," but to me it sounds like the world as it is.

In a similar vein, Bradley Campbell, a sociology professor, in referring to advocacy to recognize and eliminate microaggressions, asserted that "the movement is transforming society from a 'dignity culture,' in which people are taught to have thick skins and refuse to allow others to affect their sense of self-worth, to a 'victimhood culture' that advertises personal oppression" (Watanabe & Song, 2015, para. 9). Having "thick skin," for a person from a stereotyped group, means to just take the insults without any negative effect on self-worth. That seems to me to be condoning another underminer that saps the mental bandwidth of our students, asking them to pay the cost in achievement and potential.

Lukianoff and Haidt (2015) asked, "Would they [students] not be better prepared to flourish if we taught them to question their own emotional reactions, and to give people the benefit of the doubt?" (para. 46). It's a good question. Students might be better prepared to flourish except for the ongoing cost to mental bandwidth that is required to carry out this cognitive process. Even though these authors claimed that the process "becomes automatic" in time, no two situations are exactly alike, and some cognitive (and, yes, emotional) resources would be used up in this frequent analytical process. Another idea is to bring the struggle out in the open and help majority people develop a cognitive process of their own that involves a measure of empathy that encourages them to try to avoid perpetrating, even unintentionally, actions that feel like microaggressions to our students. Green (2016) posed the following question:

Should colleges ask historically marginalized students to become grittier and more resilient, or should their focus be directed toward achieving greater racial justice so that black students do not have to compromise their mental and physical well-being by being resilient? (para. 16)

I think the answer to the second part is "yes." The evidence is clear that racism (and classism, homophobia, etc.) has made people physically, mentally, and spiritually ill and dampened their chances at a fair shot at higher education (and at life and living). This is not a problem that non-majority people need to solve. It is for all of us, with majority people in the lead at colleges and universities, to root out this social pollution and clean up the social environment for everyone.

To emphasize once more the cumulative cost of lifelong exposure to racism, especially to modern racism, I ask you to consider that

> the accumulative stress from racial microaggressions produces racial battle fatigue. The stress of unavoidable front-line racial battles in historically white spaces leads to people of color feeling mentally, emotionally, and physically drained. The stress from racial microaggressions can become lethal when the accumulation of physiological symptoms of racial battle fatigue are untreated, unnoticed, misdiagnosed, or personally dismissed. (W. A. Smith et al., 2006, p. 301)

It is up to those of us who lead higher education institutions to recognize and try to alleviate the kinds of hostile or just "chilly" racial environments that have precluded an equitable situation for low-income and nonmajority students. Let us not accept what Harvard psychiatrist Chester Pierce called "mundane extreme environmental stress" (MEES; Carroll, 1998, p. 271) as just the way it is on our campuses. These environments, according to Pierce, are ones in which "racism and subtle oppression are ubiquitous, constant, continuing and mundane" (p. 271). Carroll (1998) described the terms as

> mundane, because this stress is so common, a part of day-to-day experience of all Blacks that it is almost taken for granted; extreme, because it has harsh impact on the psyche and world view of Blacks; environmental, because it is environmentally induced and fostered; stress, because the ultimate impact on African Americans and their families is indeed stressful, detracting and energy-consuming. (p. 271)

Even though it's easy to take the mundane as just the way it is and always will be, we can, with intention, change our institutional environments to ones in which all students can flourish and develop academically and personally to their fullest potential.

# 6

# STEREOTYPE THREAT

Black men have the lowest rates of college persistence and completion of any group in the United States. Even before college, the educational outcomes for Black males are not good. According to the Schott Foundation for Public Education (2010), only 47% of Black males graduated from high school with others in their entering class. Harper (2012a) reported that less than a third of Black men earned bachelor's degrees within six years. I suggest that a possible contributing factor is *stereotype threat*, a term first used by Claude Steele (1997) to describe "a threat in the air":

> It is the social-psychological threat that arises when one is in a situation or doing something for which a negative stereotype about one's group applies. . . . And for those who identify with the domain to which the stereotype is relevant, this predicament can be self-threatening . . . and, in several ways, hampers their achievement. (p. 614)

Steele and Aronson (1995) gave Black and White college students a difficult verbal test in one of two conditions, one in which students were told that the test was about intellectual ability, and the other in which they were told that the test was about laboratory problem-solving ability. Because there is a stereotype that Black students have lower intellectual ability than White students, the Black students in the intellectual ability condition worried that their performance would confirm that stereotype. The stress of this worry negatively affected their performance so that they scored well below what was expected by their ability. Black students in the problem-solving ability condition performed as well as their equally able White classmates. In a follow-up experiment, Steele and Aronson manipulated one simple feature, asking students in one condition to record their race on a questionnaire just before they took the test, and in the other test, no such request was made. Just this simple mention of race was enough to depress the scores of Black students. Since that time, the phenomenon has been found in many settings with different groups of people in domains in which there is high identification with the specific group about which there is a negative stereotype.

In a study involving female and male students taking a difficult math test (Spencer, Steele, & Quinn, 1999), stereotype threat theory was evident, in that women performed below their ability level. These were female students who were good at math and were highly identified with it. In another very similar experiment, female and male students were matched for their strong abilities in literature. On the difficult literature exam, females scored as well as their male counterparts; there is not a stereotype that females are not good at literature. In another experiment, females in one test condition were told that the exam would identify gender differences, and in the other test condition, they were told that it was insensitive to those differences. Only in the former condition did females score well below what was expected by their ability.

Further research on the necessary conditions for stereotype threat to depress performance was done by J. Aronson and colleagues (1999) and reported in "When White Men Can't Do Math." In the experimental condition, White students were told that there was a consistent pattern that Asian students performed better than White students in math. In the control condition, students were just told that the math exam was meant to examine the mental processes involved in doing math problems. The participants were White male students who were very good at math; their performance in math classes and their scores on standardized math tests showed their high proficiency. Before the exam, students were given a questionnaire about their level of identification with themselves as math students or how important their math ability was to their self-esteem. Within the experimental condition in which the superiority of Asian students was emphasized, only those students who were highly identified with math experienced depressed performance. This study showed us the situational nature of stereotype threat. These White men were not, in general, the subject of negative stereotypes about their academic ability, especially in math (as males are generally believed to be better at math than females). But in this case, the suggestion that another group was better at math was enough to negatively affect their performance.

There are many other studies that have replicated Steele and Aronson's (1995) findings that when a person is highly identified with an area of performance and with her or his group (race/ethnicity, gender, age, etc.) and when there is a negative stereotype about that group, the stress produced by worrying that performance will affirm the stereotype acts to decrease performance. If this is a situational experience, as with the men and the math exam, there are probably no lasting effects of the discomfort or of the lower-than-expected performance. But what about Black, Hispanic, and Native American college students who encounter daily messages that carry low expectations for their academic performance?

The long-term harm of stereotype threat for nonmajority students is that a "negative recursive cycle can occur, where psychological threat and poor performance feed off one another, leading to ever-worsening performance" (G. L. Cohen, Garcia, Apful, & Master, 2006, p. 1309). Nonmajority students who belong to groups about which there are negative stereotypes not only are more likely to be kept out of opportunities for furthering their education, because of low ACT or SAT scores, for instance, but also may quit trying once they get to college as the pressure of poor performance exacerbates their stress and causes them to give up entirely. The negative effects of stereotype threat leave members of these groups consistently underperforming, resulting in students who never enter college or drop out once they have started.

In *Whistling Vivaldi* (2010), as Steele took us on his journey with his research colleagues on the study of the stereotype threat phenomenon, he began to refer instead to "identity threat." He talked about identity "contingencies," the social stigma that we feel related to certain identities, regardless of whether there is overt racism or sexism or homophobia in the immediate environment. He emphasized that this can happen to any of us in the right conditions and that we have probably all been in situations in which we are looking around for clues that we are in an "identity safe" environment. It is in "identity threat" environments where we might underperform because of the bandwidth tax caused by a sense of hypervigilance related to confirming a negative stereotype of our identity group. First-generation and nonmajority students at predominantly White colleges and universities encounter multiple cues that they are in an identity threat situation, robbing them of mental bandwidth.

One last point on identity threat: What makes matters worse for nonmajority groups on college campuses, as Bright (2002) pointed out, is that stereotypes are more likely to affect behavior in times of some stress:

> Research has found that people are increasingly reliant on stereotypes when under stress, or when suffering from a depletion of cognitive resources (Blair & Banaji, 1996; Macrae, Milne, & Bodenhausen, 1994). It is argued that stereotype application automatically starts to unconsciously functionally dominate under these conditions in an endeavor to free up resources (Blair & Banaji, 1996; Macrae, Milne, & Bodenhausen, 1994). This finding may explain some aspects of overt racial discrimination, which is increasingly evident in poignant situations. (para. 6)

This could explain the report from a Black graduate student that on the day of the final exam in a difficult science course, his two White male tablemates, commenting clearly in his hearing, lamented the shooting death of a favorite country and western singer. They reflected that it would have been so much better if President Obama had been shot and killed. Were these White students, nervous about the test, consciously or unconsciously, trying to shore up their mental bandwidth by undermining the confidence of their Black classmate? Perhaps that was the case. But the negative effect on the Black student's already-stressed mental bandwidth was devastating, just when he needed maximum cognitive resources for the exam.

# 7

# DISIDENTIFICATION WITH ACADEMIC SELF

B ecause stereotype or identity threat can have such a depressive effect on student motivation and success, one of the most serious conse- quences is the tendency for students, as early as elementary school, to disidentify with the part of themselves that relates to academics. Humans are a resilient species; when we encounter obstacles, we figure out a way to deal with them and survive. One of the ways we keep going, psychologically, in the face of failure or negative messages is to protect our self-esteem from assault. Our self-esteem is formed from the way we feel about ourselves in a variety of domains in our life. When children live in situations of perpet- ual scarcity, the environment is often not one in which education is highly valued or in which there are adequate resources that support education. One strategy nonmajority and poor students use (sometimes unconsciously) to decrease identity threat is to base their self-esteem on domains in which they can be successful and disidentify from domains in which they have failed or in which society expects them to fail. They change their self-concept so that a particular domain (e.g., academic performance), is no longer the basis of self-esteem (J. Aronson, Fried, & Good, 2001). J. Aronson and colleagues (1998) called this tendency "a quite normal response to the low or demean- ing expectations that come to the individual in the form of cultural stereo- types" (p. 44).

This disidentification is really very functional from a survival perspec- tive. Why would people want to continue to connect their self-esteem with a domain in which they have experienced and expect to continue to experi- ence frequent failure? As any third grader would tell you, "That doesn't even make sense!" Steele (1997) told us there is evidence of this disidentification. Even though Black students as a group consistently perform below White students on standardized tests (Jaschik, 2015; Jencks & Phillips, 1998; "The Widening Racial Scoring Gap," 2016), high school completion (National

43

Center for Education Statistics, 2015), and other measures of academic performance, "their global self-esteem is as high or higher than that of white students" (Steele, 1997, p. 623). This difference in self-esteem was affirmed by later research (Bachman, O'Malley, Freedman-Doan, Trzesniewski, & Dennellan, 2011) in which over 100,000 8th-, 10th-, and 12th-grade students were followed from 1991 to 2008. Black high school students scored higher in self-esteem than did White, Hispanic, and Asian students.

An explanation for this mismatch between academic performance and self-esteem could be that Black students choose to base their self-esteem on parts of their life where they are more likely to find positive regard and success. So, instead of academics, they might look to their relationships with family or friends, sports, work, or music. Although these may be very positive areas in the life of young Black students, for those who arrive at college, this disidentification with their academic self may become a barrier to their success. Any of these activities or associations might give them a sense of belonging that they don't get at school. Regardless of the alternative identity, they have become used to devoting much of their bandwidth to nonacademic domains; their brains will need some time to readjust. They might also have very strong, positive attachments to family and friends "back home," which, although highly functional in high school and in life in general, can sometimes pull them away from their new college life and cause them to experience conflicting loyalties, robbing more mental bandwidth.

# 8

# BELONGINGNESS
# UNCERTAINTY

Integral to the cycle of poor performance leading to anxiety leading to more poor performance that may be the outcome of stereotype threat is the lack of a sense of belonging, another kind of scarcity. This sense characterizes the first-year college experience of many nonmajority students. In a 2007 study, Walton and Cohen introduced the term for the insecurity that students feel about themselves as scholars:

> Stigmatization can create a global uncertainty about the quality of one's social bonds in academic and professional domains—a state of *belongingness uncertainty*. As a consequence, events that threaten one's social connectedness, although seen as minor by other individuals, can have large effects on the motivation of those contending with a threatened social identity. (p. 94)

Before discussing *belonging* as a critical factor in college success, I want to mention two theories of sociopsychological development that are relevant. The first is Maslow's (1943) hierarchy of needs, which describes a motivational theory that asserts that we as humans must have our physiological needs for food, water, and shelter satisfied before we can think about safety and security and then about belongingness needs. This hierarchy is often shown as a pyramid (see Figure 8.1).

This theory is applicable to our discussion about the sense of belonging of first-generation and nonmajority students at colleges and universities. If students lack enough financial resources to be certain about consistent access to food, shelter, and basic health care, for instance, they won't even have the mental bandwidth to think about their sense of belonging. If they are concerned about their physical safety, for instance, in the case of LGBT students on some campuses, they also can't focus on belonging to the place.

**Figure 8.1.** Maslow's hierarchy of needs.

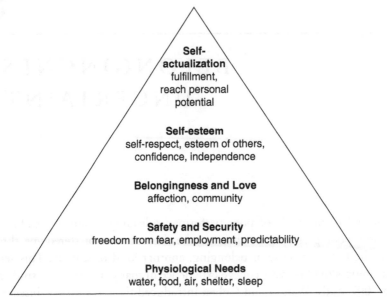

*Note.* Adapted from "A Theory of Human Motivation," by A. H. Maslow, 1943, *Psychological Review, 50,* pp. 370–396.

Thus, to the extent that we are able, we need to help students meet their basic needs so that they can move on to establishing their place in the campus culture; this sense of belonging is positively correlated with academic success.

In the second theory, Erik Erikson (Zastrow & Kirst-Ashman, 2013) proposed a theory of psychosocial development in which he described a series of psychosocial "crises" that each person has to resolve as a part of development from infancy to old age. The relevant crisis for college students just out of high school is "identity versus role confusion." Young people at this age are "finding themselves." They need to work out who they are in the context of their social world. Developing a healthy sense of self, a personal identity, requires that a person belong someplace, among some group of people. Coming to college requires, for many students, a fairly significant shift in personal identity, from son or daughter to independent college student. This is a relatively easy transition for many White, economically secure students whose parents went to college and for whom college is an expected next step after high school. First-generation and nonmajority students may not have the social or cultural capital to easily transition to college. So for them, establishing a new or enhanced identity, in the face of identity threat environments and undermining social interactions, may be a serious challenge that can require significant mental bandwidth.

In a talk at the University of Delaware in 2015, Gregory Walton discussed the things that students worry about the most: "Do I belong? Am I smart enough? Does this matter?" (B. Miller, 2015). A review of the literature on belonging leads quickly to work on *mattering* and its opposite, *marginality*. Schlossberg (1989) wrote a foundational article that addressed these two poles of belonging and how mattering is a motivator. She quoted M. Rosenberg and McCullough (1981), who said, "Mattering is a motive: the feeling that others depend on us, are interested in us, are concerned with our fate . . . exercises a powerful influence on our actions" (p. 165). Mattering is believing that we matter to someone else. That belief acts as the motivator. Bump (2016) added another aspect of mattering, which she called *reliance*. Students want to know that they matter to someone else, but they also want to be needed. Do people come to them for help or to talk when they're having a bad time, to ask for advice or for their opinion?

When students belong in a place, they have, or begin to build, *social capital*, defined as the connections, often informal, that they need to get inside information and to gain access to resources, such as tutoring or on-campus jobs. The importance of social capital is underestimated on many campuses; we make assumptions that we just have to tell students about available resources or put up flyers and they will have the wherewithal to get to and use those resources. When they don't, we might conclude that they're not good enough to be in college. After a study of support services in two urban community colleges, Karp, O'Gara, and Hughes (2008) argued that schools

> inadvertently perpetuate inequality, despite their best intentions to do the opposite. In doing so, they legitimate unequal access to postsecondary credentials by creating structures that appear to be open-access, easy to use, and fair. In other words, through the very act of offering a wide range of support services, particularly when these services are offered in an uncoordinated way, colleges perpetuate the notion that those who cannot effectively use such services are not worthy of a college degree. The locus of success or failure is shifted away from the structure of the institution and onto the student. (pp. 6–7)

The authors gave several examples of structural issues that impede progress for some students, including not requiring part-time students to take the first-year "student success" class, thus excluding them from vital information about resources and services; having general academic advisers with whom the students had no ongoing relationship and from whom they sometimes got poor advice; and having poorly advertised support services that were, in reality, unavailable for many qualified students because they didn't know about them. Students with high levels of social capital used support services at higher rates than those with medium or low levels and made steady progress toward a degree at significantly higher rates than the other two groups (100%, 36%, and 17%, respectively) (Karp et al., 2008).

T. M. Freeman, Anderman, and Jensen (2007) found that a sense of belonging was positively associated with academic success and motivation. Students who felt they belonged were more likely to see the value of the required course work. They had higher self-efficacy related to their estimates of their chances to succeed in the course.

In 1928, Robert E. Park wrote an article called "Human Migration and the Marginal Man," in which he posited that as a result of migration, a new kind of person was formed, whom he called the "marginal man." This person lived in two cultures at once, a "cultural hybrid" (p. 892). Almost 90 years later, his description applies to many of our nonmajority and first-generation students who arrive on our campuses and, in essence, enter a foreign culture:

> A man living and sharing intimately in the cultural life and traditions of two distinct peoples; never quite willing to break, even if he were permitted to do so, with his past and his traditions, and not quite accepted, because of racial prejudice, in the new society in which he now sought to find a place. (p. 892)

In the mid-1990s, I moved with my family to northern Alberta, Canada, to take on a two-year volunteer position, living out in the bush with the Lubicon Cree. The Lubicon are First Nations people who were struggling for their life against the oil and paper industries that had occupied their traditional lands in the early 1980s, essentially destroying their 2,000-year-old hunting and trapping livelihood. One of my jobs was to administer the funds from the federal government that were available to indigenous Canadians for higher education. Most young people didn't choose to go on to college or university, even though it was free for them. At first baffled by this, I learned that for this traditional land-based culture, going away to the city and getting a college degree irrevocably changed the relationship of young people with their family. I remember that Thomas Wolfe's (1940) novel *You Can't Go Home Again* took on a new meaning for me. The sense of belonging in a college setting that would be necessary for a young person's academic success meant that the foundational belonging to his or her family could be compromised beyond repair. I began to understand how for many young native people the cost of getting an education was just too high.

Students who are different from the majority on campus may struggle with finding a place to belong in college. Strayhorn (2012) did several research projects on students' sense of belonging. In a study of Latino students, he found that they reported the difficulty of balancing academic work with family demands, especially if the family was low income and the student had some responsibility to help out financially. Developing a sense of belonging on campus may be problematic for these students. In a study of gay students, Strayhorn found similar feelings of not belonging. One Black/Haitian lesbian said, "Feelings of not belonging eat at your core" (p. 39). A gay Black man described how he was stuck between two groups, belonging to neither:

> Jokingly, I tell people that if I learned anything at all, I learned that I don't matter and I may not even exist [laughing]. I mean, of course, I exist in a physical sense; I breathe, I move, I take up space. Depending on where I am, that may be all I do or not much else. Among Blacks, I'm an automatic "delete" because I'm a gay man. Among gays, I stick out like a sore thumb because I'm Black. Before I even open my mouth, people make all sorts of assumptions about me because Black is straight for a lot of people and gay is White. So, where do I fit in the puzzle? Not many places [laughing], at least not easily or without trying hard to fit. That's the truth, and like they say, the truth hurts. (p. 39)

Research consistently points to belonging as a critical factor in college success. But there are costs to belonging for first-generation and nonmajority students, and we would be wise to try to understand those costs as we encourage them to get engaged. Many students feel the social and emotional pressure that comes with educational achievement beyond what is the norm for their family or neighborhood. Cardoza (2016) explained,

> For almost 20 percent of first-generation students, English is not a first language. These students are often needed at home, simply to translate. Sometimes they feel guilty because, now that they have a high school diploma, they should get a job and help support their family. One student told me it was important for her to show that she "doesn't think she's better" than the people she's left behind. (para. 11)

Richard Rodriguez (1982) addressed this situation poignantly in "The Achievement of Desire," in which he described how his education, a joy to him, alienated him from his family:

> Here is a child who cannot forget that his academic success distances him from a life he loved, even from his own memory of himself. . . . I kept so

much, so often, to myself. Sad. Enthusiastic. Troubled by the excitement of coming upon new ideas. Eager. Fascinated by the promising texture of a brand-new book. I hoarded the pleasures of learning. Alone for hours. Enthralled. Nervous. I rarely looked away from my books—or back on my memories. Nights when relatives visited and the front rooms were warmed by Spanish sounds, I slipped quietly out of the house. (pp. 48, 51)

It is difficult for many of us who grew up in educated families in which college was an assumption to realize what some of our students are sacrificing for the opportunity to come to college and get a degree.

When it comes to a sense of belonging in college, many first-generation and nonmajority students are in a catch-22. To be academically successful, they need to belong at least to some extent. The price, however, in the potential damage to family relationships discourages their deep engagement with school and with their academic self. For those students who persist, the bandwidth tax of this persistent belongingness struggle can seriously affect academic performance.

# 9

# FOCUS ON LGBT STUDENTS

R ecently, I facilitated a workshop on my campus for instructors and staff who work with students whose academic profiles indicate that they might need extra support to succeed in college. When a conversation began about LGBT students, I had a sudden realization that the bandwidth tax of pretending (even some of the time) that you are not what you really are must be tremendous and almost unimaginable to a straight, cisgender person (someone whose sense of gender matches sex assignment at birth). So, even though this group of students is included in the discussions of the effects of poverty and racism (and other "differentisms"), LGBT students face a unique set of challenges that are not shared by the other groups. (Sometimes, the abbreviation LGBTQ is used. The "Q" can refer to *questioning*, for people who are in the process of identity formation around affectional orientation or gender identity, or *queer*, a term that has been reclaimed by some people to represent the entire range of gender–relationship nonconformity.)

According to the American College Health Association–National College Health Assessment of Fall 2015, 11.6% of over 93,000 college student respondents from 108 institutions in the United States reported being lesbian, gay, bisexual, or questioning, and 0.4% reported that they were transgender. To the extent that homophobia, transphobia ("dislike of or prejudice against transsexual or transgender people") (Transphobia, n.d.), and differentism result in LGBT students experiencing higher levels of stress, physical and mental ill health, and lower socioeconomic status, they very likely have the same depletion of mental bandwidth as their straight and cisgender peers. According to the Healthy People 2020 (2016) report, "Research suggests that LGBT individuals face health disparities linked to societal stigma, discrimination, and denial of their civil and human rights." I want to give attention to the lived reality of LGBT students, beginning with the fact that there is so much misinformation and misunderstanding about sexual orientation and gender identity. One of the respondents to a Human Rights Campaign survey said, "I live in such a narrow-minded community—it's really hard on me. I deal with so much ignorance on a daily basis" (Human Rights Campaign, 2012).

It is important that we understand the terms, some old and some new, related to sexual and gender relationships and identities. Table 9.1 lists some of them, although there are others currently in use, and new terms are emerging as people continue to define themselves outside of what used to be a set of strict binary systems.

Why are LGBT college students at extra risk compared to their poor and racially and ethnically diverse peers? J. David Macey (personal

**TABLE 9.1**
**Sexual Orientation and Gender Identity Terms and Definitions**

| Term | Definition |
|---|---|
| **Sexual Orientation** | |
| *Lesbian* | Women who are emotionally, romantically, or sexually attracted to other women. |
| *Gay* | Persons who are emotionally, romantically, or sexually attracted to persons of the same gender. |
| *Bisexual* | Persons who are emotionally, romantically, or sexually attracted to more than one sex, gender or gender identity, though not necessarily simultaneously, in the same way or to the same degree. |
| *Asexual* | The lack of sexual attraction to or desire for any group. (It is different from *celibacy*, which is a deliberate abstention from sexual activity.) |
| **Gender Identity** | |
| *Transgender woman* | A person who identifies as a woman who was assigned a male identity at birth (MTF: "male-to-female") |
| *Transgender man* | A person who identifies as a man who was assigned a female identity at birth (FTM: "female-to-male") |
| *Transsexual* | A medical tem referring to transgender people, related to sex-affirmation treatment. |
| *Trans* | Short for *transgender* (and *transsexual*) and sometimes is an umbrella term for people who identify anywhere along the gender-variant spectrum. |
| *Cisgender* | People for whom their sense of their gender matches their sex assignment at birth. |

*(Continues)*

TABLE 9.1 *(Continued)*

| Term | Definition |
|------|------------|
| *Gender nonconforming* | Cisgender people whose gender expression is not validated by the dominant culture (e.g., a male who primarily expresses as feminine in behavior and/or appearance). |
| *Agender* | People who don't identify as having a gender. |
| *Genderqueer* | Gender identity falls outside the binary of female–male. |
| *Genderfluid* | Gender identity and/or expression changes across time and situation. |
| *Crossdresser* | People who are comfortable with their physical body but enjoy dressing like the opposite gender. |
| *Two spirit* | From indigenous American culture, the term *two spirit* describes trans or gender nonconforming people, although there are much more complex, tribe-defined nuances to this term. (Having fallen out of use, as it was an identity that was especially oppressed during colonization, it has been reclaimed. Two spirit people were seen in a very positive light in some indigenous cultures.) |
| **Biological Variant** | |
| *Intersex* | Biological/physical sex at birth does not fit the typical characteristics of either female or male (also *androgynous* or *hermaphrodite*, which refer specifically to a person who has both female and male reproductive organs). |

*Note.* Adapted from the following four sources: *Transgender: Understanding Gender Differences* (brochure, Title No. 374), by K. Clark and M. Quackenbush, 2014, Scotts Valley, CA: ETR Associates; "Some Very Basic Tips for Making Higher Education Accessible to Trans Students and Rethinking the Way We Talk About Gendered Bodies," by D. Spade, 2011, *Radical Teacher, 92*, pp. 57–62, 80; *LGBTQIA Resource Center Glossary*, by LGBTQIA Resource Center, 2016, University of California–Davis; and Human Rights Campaign, n.d.

communication, October 6, 2016), an English professor and long-time adviser with a campus LGBT student group, emphasized the "sense of profound isolation and alienation" among LGBT students, even those who have relatively supportive families:

> Whereas many (even most) young people from non-majority backgrounds are reared in family contexts in which they share their non-majority identity with their immediate family members, LGBT youth are almost always reared by heterosexual, cisgender parents, with heterosexual, cisgender siblings and extended family members. . . . Youth from less privileged

socio-economic positions will almost inevitably share with their immediate family members the experience of socio-economic deprivation and marginalization. LGBT youth, however, may well wonder whether anyone shares their experience and may lack any role models (whether positive or negative) who could help them to explore what it means to be an LGBT person and to recognize the opportunities (otherwise largely invisible to youth) available to LGBT persons.

In addition, it seems like there are four other ways that students in this population are especially vulnerable. First, except for economically secure White gay men, every other person in an LGBT group experiences *intersectionality* which means that his or her identity includes both LGBT and at least one other characteristic that puts him or her in a negatively stereotyped group; for instance, a Black lesbian, a Hispanic gay man, or a poor bisexual woman. When two nonmajority, low socioeconomic status identities are in combination, the challenges are multiplied, as LaSala and Frierson (2012) so clearly articulated in the case of Black gay men. Second, because of widespread ignorance and misinformation, LGBT students might not only be discriminated against or hated because of their identities but also *blamed* for them. Even though racial hatred continues in the United States, no one blames a person for being Black or Latino or Native American. People are sometimes blamed for being poor, but not in the same way as a transgender person or a lesbian is blamed, because so many people believe that these are "lifestyle choices." Third, in a patriarchal society that is dominated by White, straight men and their rules and unquestioned superiority, people who refuse to conform to the Western gender and sexual binary, within a system in which women as a group are subordinate to men as a group, pose a serious threat to the entire enterprise. Fourth, although changes are happening in several mainline denominations in the United States, homosexuality has been and is still seen as sinful and unacceptable by most religious groups (Masci & Lipka, 2015). Our students may carry emotional scars from having been banned from or ostracized within the churches in which they were raised. In addition, for students growing up in the midst of so many anti-LGBT attitudes and messages, internalized oppression may continue to be a factor during the college years (Chollar, 2013). For these reasons and others, LGBT students are very likely to arrive in our classrooms and on our campuses with a multitude of stresses and daily challenges that result in depleted mental bandwidth.

As LGBT youth come out of high school and enter our colleges and universities, how might their life experiences affect their current readiness to succeed, academically and otherwise? According to the Centers for Disease Control and Prevention (Centers for Disease Control and Prevention, 2014),

"Most lesbian, gay, bisexual, transgender, and questioning youth are happy and thrive during their adolescent years, [but] . . . they are more likely than their heterosexual peers to experience difficulties in their lives and school environments." They are more likely than their straight peers to have experienced violence, including "bullying, teasing, harassment, physical assault, and suicide-related behaviors" (Coker, Austin, & Schuster, 2010). Because of discrimination and ostracism, many LGBT youth feel disaffected from their families, neighborhoods, and schools. In a study of 10,000 LGBT youth from ages 13 to 17 years from all regions of the United States, the Human Rights Campaign (HRC; 2012) found an overrepresentation of this group among youth who are homeless, in foster care, and living in risky situations. Although, in general, they are resilient and look forward to a more positive future, they face significant life challenges that can have lifelong effects on their health and well-being. While non-LGBT youth are worrying about their grades, college or career, finances to go to college, and appearance, LGBT youth are concerned about their families not accepting them, being bullied, being found out, being hated or misunderstood, and where they can safely live. Contrary to the CDC report (Centers for Disease Control and Prevention, 2014), non-LGBT youth are almost twice as likely to say that they are happy (67%) than are LGBT youth (38%). Almost a third (29%) of LGBT youth say that they don't have an adult with whom they can talk about personal problems, compared to only 17% of non-LGBT youth. Over half (52%) of LGBT youth report that they have used alcohol and drugs compared to just 22% of non-LGBT youth. (Although the Human Rights Campaign survey didn't report tobacco use, the CDC [2015] estimated that cigarette smoking prevalence was 23.9% among lesbian, gay, and bisexual people compared to 16.6% among heterosexuals.) This comprehensive Human Rights Campaign study revealed many other ways in which the lives of LGBT youth can be negatively affected by the stigma related to their identities. According to a publication from the California Community Colleges Student Mental Health Program (n.d.),

> The two factors known to be most detrimental to LGBTQ student mental health are hostile school climate and family rejection. Both are associated with increases in rates of homelessness, substance abuse, suicide, and unsafe sexual behavior among LGBTQ youth (Toomey, Ryan, Diaz, Card, & Russell, 2010). Being bullied at school doubles the risk of suicide and is associated with increased depression, decreased self-esteem, increased substance use, and increased school dropout (Fedewa & Ahn, 2011; Russell & Toomey, 2012). Being rejected at home increases the risk of depression more than six times and increases the risk of suicide more than eight times (Ryan, Huebner, Diaz, & Sanchez, 2009). (p. 1)

These persistent threats for LGBT students remind me of Pierce's MEES (Carroll, 1998): "For many LGBT and gender non-conforming adolescents, the simple, daily routine of going to school is fraught with harassment and victimization" (Russell, Ryan, Toomey, Diaz, & Sanchez, 2011, p. 223). It is like the "wearying drone of negativity" (C. Thompson, 2008) that characterizes modern racism for a Māori man in New Zealand. Even "coming out" (telling family, friends, and others about one's LGBT identity), sometimes thought of as a singular event, is actually an ongoing process; a new decision has to be made in each situation as to whether or not to be honest about one's identity (Chollar, 2013). As a result of being in a constant state of stress and vigilance, LGBT students may experience deterioration in physical and mental health, a critical factor in reducing mental bandwidth.

Before discussing some specific ways that we can create safe and supportive environments for LGBT students, I want to give a bit of attention to the "T." Trans and gender nonconforming people may be the least understood group among the five. J. M. Grant, Mottet, and Tanis (2011), after a national study of discrimination against trans people, concluded,

> Transgender and gender non-conforming people face injustice at every turn: in childhood homes, in school systems that promise to shelter and educate, in harsh and exclusionary workplaces, at the grocery store, the hotel front desk, in doctors' offices and emergency rooms, before judges and at the hands of landlords, police officers, health care workers and other service providers. (p. 1)

From survey responses of 6,450 trans and gender nonconforming people in the United States, J. M. Grant and colleagues (2011) found that the most serious discrimination was experienced by people of color, with Black respondents faring the worst of all the race/ethnicity groups. Many respondents live in poverty; they are four times more likely than those in the general population to have annual household incomes less than $10,000. Forty-one percent of respondents reported attempting suicide compared to 1.6% of the general population. Almost half (47%) reported that they had been not hired, denied a promotion, or fired because they were trans or gender non-conforming. Most respondents (71%) said that they had avoided discrimination by hiding their gender or gender transition, which is especially tragic when 78% reported that they were more comfortable at work and their performance improved after they had transitioned. The report has many further details about discrimination in public accommodations, abuse by police and in prison, discrimination in health care, poor health outcomes, and other serious negative experiences. Higher education institutions must be very intentional in becoming informed about these issues and nurturing these unique students so they can be successful in school, work, and life.

In Part Three, I share many interventions and ideas that show promise of helping students gain back the mental bandwidth lost to poverty and racism (including differentism, homophobia, and transphobia). Before that, however, I want to share a few of the critical factors in support of LGBT students.

According to the CDC (2014), "For youth to survive in their schools and communities, they need to feel socially, emotionally, and physically safe and supported" (para. 8). That could be said for all students, of course, and nurturing a sense of belonging and being valued for their whole set of identities is crucial. Several areas in which we can create positive environments for LGBT students include offering welcoming and inclusive policies and practices, setting standards for appropriate behavior, providing comprehensive mental and physical health referrals and support, and incorporating practices that reduce social isolation (California Community Colleges Student Mental Health Program, n.d.). (A note on mental health services: We don't want to communicate to LGBT students that their identity equals mental illness and assume that every one of them needs mental health services. However, because of the stresses outlined previously, many LGBT students might need support from mental health professionals.) Some campuses have in-person or online training to educate the university community about LGBT issues and how to create supportive environments. "Safe-Zone" or similar programs provide more in-depth training to faculty, staff, and administrators about the realities of life for LGBT students and ways to become visible allies, often by displaying a symbol on office doors that indicates a safe space.

To reduce isolation, campuses can encourage student support groups and clubs that help LGBT students connect with each other and the larger community and get experience in organizational and leadership development. Sometimes groups are focused on LGBT issues, and others might invite these students to relate around other activities such as sports, activism, art, religion, or a specific academic discipline. Faculty and staff LGBT associations can be important resources for students and offer mentoring, guidance, and the assurance of acceptance. There are alumni groups and private foundations (e.g., the Point Foundation, www.pointfoundation.org) that offer scholarships and mentoring to students. On some campuses, there are resource centers, gathering places, or housing options for LGBT students. The Trevor Project (www.thetrevorproject.org) offers online resources on suicide prevention and crisis intervention.

Specifically for trans students, the Transgender Law and Policy Institute (www.transgenderlaw.org) has ample resources about how we can provide fair and equal treatment of trans people. The institute reminds us of several questions, including the following: Can a student add a preferred name to university documents and class rosters? Do forms that ask for gender have choices other than female and male? Are there gender-inclusive restrooms on campus? Does the institution have policies that allow trans people to join gender-segregated student organizations?

Dean Spade (2011), at the Seattle University School of Law, gave us some excellent guidelines that help us create learning environments that are inclusive of all people. His article gave additional details, but the following list includes some of his suggestions:

- When establishing class guidelines, include something like "It is important that this classroom be a respectful environment where everyone can participate comfortably. One part of this is that everyone should be referred to by the name they prefer, the correct pronunciation of their name, and the pronoun they prefer, like *she, ze, he,* or *they.*"
- Avoid calling the roll or otherwise reading the roster aloud until you have given students a chance to state their preferred name.
- Allow students to choose what name they prefer to use and what pronouns they prefer. If the class is a reasonable size, you might have each student make a name badge or table tent (mine might look like the one in Figure 9.1).
- When facilitating a class discussion, ask people to identify their pronouns when they introduce themselves.
- Avoid asking personal questions of LGBT students that you would not ask of any student.

**Figure 9.1.** Cia's name badge.

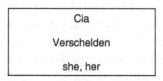

Beyond these specific ideas, in Part Three, I share ideas of interventions and other important issues of social environments that can help economically insecure and nonmajority students recover mental bandwidth so they are more ready to learn and develop.

# PART THREE

## INTERVENTIONS THAT MITIGATE THE NEGATIVE EFFECTS OF POVERTY AND THE UNDERMINERS

*They started with the assumption that nothing was wrong with the students.*

—Stephanie Fryberg, University of Washington (B. Miller, 2015)

To summarize, poverty and racism (and differentism more generally) rob our students of mental bandwidth so they have limited cognitive resources for learning. Poor people are physically and mentally less healthy than people who have adequate resources; they suffer the physical consequences of chronic stress. People who experience racism every day experience similar stress and negative health outcomes. Physical and mental illness take up mental bandwidth, leaving less available for everything else, such as making good choices, being effective workers or parents, and learning.

In the United States, at least, if the political will were there, we could eliminate the worst economic inequality within current structures of taxation, commerce, and labor. We could change the way we fund public schools so that every child would have the opportunity for high-quality primary and secondary education. Every child could have an adequate diet as well as exercise and intellectual stimulation. Ending racism, classism, homophobia, and other underminers may be a bit more difficult, considering how deeply they are embedded in the culture. But for now, poverty and racism diminish the life chances of the majority of children and adolescents in the United States, many of whom will arrive at institutions of higher education in the near future. Acknowledging the fact that many of them will have depleted mental bandwidth, we must develop strategies to help them recover cognitive resources for learning.

Research has demonstrated how changing the circumstances of a situation, sometimes through seemingly minor interventions, can have dramatic effects on the academic performance of students in nonmajority groups. Cohen and Garcia (2014) reminded us that the original Latin meaning of "to educate" is "to draw out." When we apply interventions to help students, we're not adding anything to their intelligence or giving them some kind of advantage; rather, we are trying to draw out what is already inside them that has been inhibited by exposure to sociopsychological underminers. David Yeager said, "Ultimately a person has within themselves some kind of capital, some kind of asset, like knowledge or confidence. And if we can help bring that out, they then carry that asset with them to the next difficulty in life" (Tough, 2014, para. 61). In the following chapters, I present some interventions that have shown promise in helping students recover their mental bandwidth and increase their level of learning and persistence in higher education.

# 10

# GROWTH MIND-SET

One simple intervention involves informing students of Carol Dweck's two theories of intelligence: *incremental* and *entity*. The former sees intelligence as malleable—the brain grows with new learning—whereas the latter sees intelligence as fixed (Moore & Shaughnessy, 2012). Dweck also referred to the former perspective as a *growth mind-set* and the latter as a *fixed mind-set*. Table 10.1 shows some of the beliefs of people who are operating from the two mind-sets.

The key is the belief that we can grow our brain by hard work and persistence. Making mistakes and figuring out where we went wrong and trying again and again until we solve a problem is how we grow our brain. Having a growth mind-set changes the conversation from "I'm not smart enough" and "I'm not college material" to "Give me challenges and give me support and I'll keep trying until I reach my learning goal."

Connecting this concept to stereotype threat, J. Aronson, Fried, and Good (2001) pointed out that students who were worried about confirming a negative stereotype might choose undemanding tasks on which they will surely succeed, especially when these tasks were evaluative, and they tended to devalue ability domains in which they might perform poorly.

> We suspect that negative ability stereotypes may derive part of their power to undermine intellectual performance and motivation precisely because they imply a self-threatening and inalterable deficiency—a fixed lack of intelligence. (p. 116)

J. Aronson and colleagues' (2001) idea was that one way to help students avoid responding to stereotype threat by focusing on performance was to convince them that their intelligence is expandable, that they can grow their brain by hard work and persistence. In one study, these researchers taught Black and White students about the expandability of intelligence and had them write about the concept to middle school students. Students in a control group

TABLE 10.1

**Growth Mind-Set Beliefs and Fixed Mind-Set Beliefs**

| Growth Mind-Set Beliefs | Fixed Mind-Set Beliefs |
| --- | --- |
| People can change how "smart" they are by learning new things and growing their brains. | People are born as smart as they'll ever be; intelligence is a fixed quality. |
| With hard work and effort, anyone can learn and do just about anything. | Hard work and effort are futile; if a person is not good at something, that's just the way it is. |
| No matter how smart people seem, they can still learn and improve their knowledge and skills. | Even really smart people can't get any smarter; it's just the way they were born. |
| People may seem to have certain characteristics, but they can change them with hard work and effort. | You're a certain kind of person, and you can't change that. |
| The smartest people work really hard, studying and practicing, so they can grow their brains and improve their skills. | Only people who aren't very smart or skilled have to work really hard, like doing homework or practicing music or sports. |
| It's in facing new challenges and learning new things that the most growth happens in our brains. | Challenges are just frustrating and defeating; it's better to stick with the things for which you have natural talent. |
| The most important thing is to learn and grow; mistakes are just part of the process. | If a person tries something new and fails, people will know he or she is not smart. |
| Only if people give each other constructive feedback about their work can we know where we need to improve and work to do it. | People shouldn't criticize others; it just makes them feel bad about themselves, and, anyway, they can't help it if they make mistakes. |

*Note.* Adapted from *Mindset: The New Psychology of Success,* by C. Dweck, 2006, New York, NY: Ballantine Books.

wrote "pen pal" letters, and another group didn't write letters. Both Black and White students in the growth mind-set group had significantly higher academic year GPAs than students in either of the control groups. Black, but not White, students in this group reported increased engagement and identification with school. The articulation of the growth mind-set through the writing task seems key; as students produce a persuasive argument, they may themselves be internalizing the message more deeply (Tough, 2014).

Good, Aronson, and Inzlicht (2003) examined these issues in a study with four groups of seventh graders. To the first group, they provided information about the expandability of the brain with mental work and to a second group they provided assurance that learning difficulties were normal in transition times but that they decrease as students settle into their new environment. A third group got a combination of these two messages, and a fourth group, the control group, got a neutral anti-drug use message. The measures were scores on standardized math and reading tests. In the growth mind-set condition, all students' scores increased on the math test, but the increase was more pronounced in the female students, which is consistent with what we know about the effects of stereotype threat. The gender gap in math scores disappeared when students got the nonpejorative message about learning difficulties and when they received the growth mind-set message. Students who heard the growth mind-set message had higher reading scores compared to students in the control group. This makes sense, as 80% of the students were Black or Hispanic and so were likely to have experienced stereotype threat in this domain.

Blackwell, Trzesniewski, and Dweck (2007) conducted eight weekly workshops with seventh-grade Black and Hispanic students, teaching study skills and the concept of the growth mind-set as a way to motivate them to work hard and not give up in response to setbacks. Students were taught that our brain grows with challenge and effort, which encouraged them to keep trying even if they didn't succeed the first time. A control group of students was taught only study skills in similar workshops. At the end of the academic year, the students in the control group showed a decline in math grades, which was the norm at this school, but the students in the growth mind-set group had significantly improved math grades (by 0.30 grade points).

Instructors who want to communicate an emphasis on a growth mind-set need to be clear that it's not about the grade but about the quality of the learning. The reality for most of us in higher education is that we are responsible for giving students grades based on their performance. Other factors may influence the grade, such as effort, contribution to group learning, attendance in class, improvement over time, and so on. Ultimately, however, course grades should reflect a student's grasp of the learning outcomes for the course. The students demonstrate this grasp through assignments, exams, projects, and other graded activities. Williams (2013), in talking about increasing motivation by fostering a growth mind-set, asked, "Are students given an opportunity to make up for initially low performance by putting in extra effort or figuring out how to better solve a problem?"

To apply the idea of giving students the chance to make up for early low performance and to maintain the focus on learning and persistence throughout the semester, some instructors use the following method. The instructor gives three exams, which each cover specific knowledge or application of knowledge, and a comprehensive final. The final consists of items from each of the three groups covered by the earlier exams. If a student does better on any of these groups of questions than she did on the original exam, the instructor substitutes the score on the final on that group of questions for the original exam score. What is communicated with this practice is that what matters is that the student has mastered the content by the end of the semester; there is no penalty for the earlier failure, so the student is motivated to keep learning throughout the entire semester. The concept of basing a grade on a student's best work rather than on an average of all the work done over a semester is called "standards-based" grading. Grades are expressions of the achievement of learning goals only; the question is the extent to which the student has demonstrated mastery of each of the learning goals, no matter when that demonstration happens. Townsley (2014) explained standards-based grading in detail, which includes many chances for students to demonstrate learning, including revisions and redos, and students are given multiple opportunities to practice the standard independently and in class with others. Well-articulated learning goals are given to students at the outset so that expectations are clear.

## Neurobics

To help students "grow" their brain, we can assign them neurobic exercises, with guided reflection. *Neurobics (neuron + aerobics)* are stretching exercises to increase oxygen and give our brain's neurons more life by experiencing or participating in some new activity, situation, or event. According to Jim Watson (1988), who created the original version of the assignment, when we stretch our mind, it never returns to its previous shape. Research has indicated that taxing the brain (making it "sweat") with unfamiliar exercises can improve our ability to learn, remember, and solve problems. After a very short lecture on Dweck's mind-sets, I required students in a first-year orientation class to complete four neurobic exercises over the semester. (See assignment in Appendix 10A.) Their reflections showed some trivial and some significant learning and, more important, suggested that most of them discovered that taking a risk was worth it for the new experience and insights. Some students did adventurous (to them) things such as staying up all night to see the stars and the sunrise, eating alone in a restaurant, or talking to three people they didn't know each day for a week. Other students tried changing to healthier habits such as drinking water instead of soda for a week, walking instead of skateboarding, or going to a yoga class with a friend. Many of their reflections were about how nervous they were or how they didn't think they could do the thing and then that they could do it and how good that felt. It was like they were actually feeling their brain growing, and they liked that sensation.

## "Not Yet" Versus "Not" Feedback

To help us give students the kind of feedback that encourages a growth mind-set, Dweck (2014, video) talked about the difference between the messages in "not" and "not yet." Feedback that indicates to students that they can achieve the learning outcome with more effort (knowledge, experience, focus) is more productive than the kind of feedback that says, "You're not good enough." Instructors can give students second tries, frequent specific feedback, and consistent support, practices that seem to be especially effective for first-generation and nonmajority students. Williams, Paunesku, Haley, and Sohl-Dickstein (2013) found that the kind of feedback to students made significant differences in learning outcomes in online classes. They found that the most important emphasis for producing measurably improved outcomes was that intelligence is malleable; for example, "Remember, the more you practice the smarter you become!"

## Self-Esteem Versus Self-Efficacy

In a seminar in Glasgow in 2008 (Centre for Confidence, 2008), Carol Dweck reminded us of the difference between self-concept or self-esteem and self-efficacy. Sometimes students seem to have a positive self-concept, meaning that they think they are smart and show outward confidence. As a result of going to an elite school or being a member of a certain group or from childhood messages about ability or performance, some students have what Dweck called an "empty self-belief" (Centre for Confidence, 2008, p. 2) of confidence and superiority. She related this to a fixed mind-set that is about feeling good about yourself, often by comparing yourself with the low achievement of others. What is important, she said, for a growth mind-set is to have the courage and determination to make mistakes and work to correct them. She said that self-efficacy, which is necessary for ongoing academic achievement, comes from mastery of problems through persistence, not from self-esteem. This might sound strange to some of us who have been told that we want to make students feel good about themselves by giving them positive feedback. What students need is honest and constructive feedback accompanied by assurances that they can reach their learning goals with effort and practice.

Christopher O'Neal (2014), from the UCLA Griffin School of Medicine, pointed out, "Negative self-efficacy equals lower academic performance, lower degrees of optimism, poorer health, higher stress, and higher attrition" (Prezi slide 20). He suggested the following four strategies to build self-efficacy in our students:

1. Seeing a peer succeed at a task
2. Using verbal persuasion and affirmations
3. Reducing stress and anxiety
4. Using collaborative, conceptual, and creative pedagogies (Prezi slides 26–29)

## High-Hope Syllabi

In an article on hope theory, Grasgreen (2012) referred to work at Chaffey College, where Laura Hope, dean of instructional support, is working with faculty to help them create learning environments that inspire students and give them hope. She referred to "low-hope" syllabi that are "packed with challenging assignments but with no advice or offers to help." Instructors are encouraged to examine their syllabi for "high hope," such as challenging assignments with support. An example might be a major research paper for which the student first turns in a proposal, then an outline, and then the paper, with feedback from the instructor at each step. On high-hope syllabi, expectations are clear and clarifying questions are encouraged. Grading criteria are explicit; rubrics can help communicate that clarity.

For instance, Appendix 10B shows the description and grading criteria for a short service-learning project in a sociology class. The high-hope features of this assignment are as follows:

- A proposal is submitted, and the student gets feedback.
- Grading criteria for the proposal and the reflection are very clear and included in a rubric.
- Students can work alone or with other students.
- The amount of time a student is expected to devote to the service is clearly stated.

High-hope syllabi openly offer help and support, seen in the following statement under "Expectation of the Instructor":

I will attempt to create and maintain a classroom atmosphere in which you feel free to both listen to others and express your views and ask questions to increase your learning. Please talk with me before or after class or make an appointment to see me in my office if there is anything you want to discuss or about which you are unclear. I want to be supportive of your learning and growth.

Invitational statements assure students that they are safe in a class and that the instructor is committed to the class meeting the learning needs of each student. For instance, consider the following from the "Expectations for Students" section:

I appreciate straightforward feedback from you regarding how well the class is meeting your needs. Let me know if material is not clear or when its relevance to the student learning outcomes for the course is not apparent (or if you're bored out of your mind!). It is also expected that you will treat classmates with respect, avoiding gratuitous arguments and observing the rules of confidentiality regarding personal information shared in class. See Course Ground Rules.

Major assignments on a high-hope syllabus come with *scaffolding*—a large project divided into manageable pieces, with feedback at each step. For instance, a research project might be broken down into the following components:

- Topic proposal due September 15; feedback by September 22
- Outline with six peer-reviewed journal references due by October 1; feedback by October 8
- First draft of paper due November 1; feedback by November 15
- Second/final draft of paper due by December 6

In a study of students with historically poor performance in math (Bandura & Schunk, 1981), students were split into two groups. For one group, the learning goals for the seven-session, self-directed math program were presented as large and distant—42 pages to be completed by the end of the sessions. For the other group, the goals were presented in smaller and proximal terms, completing six pages in each of seven sessions. The students in the proximal group expressed higher confidence in their math skills and scored almost twice as high on the final exam as students in the other group. The authors concluded, "When goals are proximal and seen as attainable, each completed step seems an accomplishment on its own and fuels engagement" (Cohen & Garcia, 2014, p. 15).

Last about syllabi is the issue of deadlines. In my experience, even though I am conscientious about including clear learning outcomes statements, classroom expectations, encouragement, and so on, students go right for the page with the assignments and the deadlines. Their main concern is what they have to do to get out of the course in one piece and, ideally, with a decent grade. Most faculty with whom I've worked for decades emphasize the importance of strict deadlines for assigned work. In contrast, Ellen Boucher (2016), history faculty at Amherst College, suggested that a bit of grace might be more helpful than rigidity. She asserted that students have multiple competing responsibilities that can leave them feeling overwhelmed; economically insecure students and nonmajority students, who may already have depleted bandwidth, are especially vulnerable. She argued, "Strict deadlines only serve to reproduce the inequalities of access and inclusion that universities are trying so hard to correct" (para. 6). After years of punitive lateness rules, she reworked her policy.

> Now every student in my courses can elect to take a two-day grace period on any paper—no questions asked. If, at the end of that period, they are still having trouble completing the assignment, they must meet with me in person to go over an outline of their ideas and set a schedule for getting the paper done. . . . The results have been amazing. Since changing my policy, I've seen higher-quality work, less anxiety, and fewer cases of burnout. Most of my students do take the grace period occasionally throughout the semester, but the great majority complete their assignment by the end of the two days. And when students are having serious difficulties, there is a support system in place to integrate them back into the classroom. (Boucher, 2016, para. 9, 10)

It seems to me that grace—an old-fashioned concept—might help to infuse hope into a syllabus and increase the growth mind-set and mental bandwidth of our students who most need both.

## Hope

The concept of hope is broader, of course, than what we can communicate in a syllabus. Snyder and his colleagues wrote about hope theory in 1991 and developed a scale to measure hope in college students. The Adult Hope Scale consists of 12 items that measure two characteristics, *agency* and *pathway*. Agency items relate to the energy students think they have to reach their goals, and pathway items ask students to rate their ability to figure out a way to get to the goals. More recently, some institutions have looked more closely at hope as an indicator, both how hope scores might predict academic success and how to increase hope in students who have low scores.

   In various studies over the past 20 years, for instance, high-hope students graduated at rates 13% higher than low-hope students (Snyder et al.,

2002), hope in first-semester law school students predicted academic success and greater life satisfaction after the first semester (Rand, Martin, & Shea, 2011), and hope was a better predictor of academic success than intelligence, personality, or previous scholarly achievement (Day, Hanson, Maltby, Proctor, & Wood, 2010).

At the Rose-Hulman Institute of Technology, the admissions office is using a related concept called *locus of control* as a noncognitive indicator in admission decisions. Locus of control is the extent to which students think they can control their own fate. In other words, do they have their own agency and access to pathways to reach their goals? In correlational studies at Rose-Hulman, successful academic performance was positively related to locus of control attitudes (Jaschik, 2014).

Given the apparent positive relationship between hope and academic success, are there ways we can help students increase their levels of hope? According to Grasgreen (2012), hope is innate, to a certain extent, but some experts say, "Train a student to visualize their goals, to see how they'll achieve them, even when obstacles arise, and hope will follow" (para. 6). Oklahoma State University's Learning and Student Success Opportunity (LASSO) Center is working with "at-risk" students, teaching them that they can overcome obstacles and succeed. Robert J. Sternberg, a psychologist and formerly the provost and senior vice president at Oklahoma State University, advocates helping students develop a purpose in life instead of just amassing a big knowledge base. "For me, the whole university is based around this notion that we're not just trying to teach kids a lot of facts and how to analyze those facts, but how to create meaningful lives" (Grasgreen, 2012, para. 22). Laura Hope, dean of instructional support, encouraged Chaffey College faculty to attend a summer institute on teaching strategies to promote high hope (Grasgreen, 2012). Faculty developed instructional techniques that help students see themselves as agents of their own success or failure. At Santa Clara University, Feldman and Dreher (2012) led students through a workshop on hope and how to think in more helpful ways to try to increase their hopeful, goal-directed thinking. Using Snyder's Adult Hope Scale as a pre- and posttest of effect, they found that students who participated in the workshop showed a greater increase in their hope score compared to students in a control group and reported greater progress toward one of their goals one month after the workshop.

In another study of goal setting, undergraduate students who were experiencing academic difficulties participated in an online goal-setting exercise in which they were asked to set specific personal goals and to work out the strategies to achieve them. In the following semester, compared to a control group that did other online exercises, the goal-setting group had increased GPAs, were more likely to maintain a full course load, and had reduced self-reported negative affect (Morisano, Hirsh, Peterson, Pihl, &

Shore, 2010). Might this exercise in goal-setting as college students have increased these students' identification with their academic selves? H. Grant and Dweck (2003), in a series of five studies with college students, found that setting active *learning* goals, rather than *performance* goals, "predicted active coping, sustained motivation, and higher achievement in the face of challenge" (p. 541).

The following tips are selected from Snyder's (2006, para. 11) list for helping adults increase their levels of hope. Some of these might be helpful for college students.

## Goal Tips

- Set a goal because it is something you really want, not what another wants for you.
- Make goals that stretch you in that they are set at a somewhat higher level than previous performance.
- Rank goals from most to least important.
- Select a few most important goals on which to work.
- Be sure to set aside sufficient time for the important goals.

## Pathways Tips

- Make several paths to each of your goals.
- Take long-range goals and break them down into steps.
- Start with the first step.
- Mentally go over what you would do if you run into a blockage.
- Ask for help from others in planning how to get to a desired goal.

## Agency Tips

- Learn how to talk to yourself in positive voices (e.g., "I can do this!").
- View problems as challenges.
- Learn to laugh at yourself, and enjoy a good laugh with your friends.
- Enjoy getting to your goals as much as reaching them.
- Get enough sleep.

Anyone can use these growth mind-set interventions as long as they use them in a spirit of facilitating learning. Students who arrive in the college classroom with very limited bandwidth for learning need empathy, flexibility, and high standards. They need expectations to be high and the promise of help and support to be obvious and openly offered. They need instructors and student affairs professionals with growth mind-sets who are willing to work alongside them until they find the learning and development style that works for them. They need affirmation of effort and assurance that they will be supported until the effort results in new neural pathways that make them "smarter" and more able to learn on their own. All of these attitudes and behaviors on the part of instructors not only will benefit students who arrive with diminished bandwidth but also are very likely to be good for many other students as well.

Yeager and Walton (2011) discussed a few cautions in scaling up some of the interventions. They emphasized that it's the psychological experience created by the intervention that should be replicated, not the specifics of the intervention. When we talk with students about a growth mind-set, it is so they will be able to rebound from early setbacks, not so they will become knowledgeable about the function of the human brain. People who try to convince students of the merits of a growth mind-set and yet consistently demonstrate a fixed mind-set might not be very successful.

# Neurobic Exercises

Personal growth and brain growth happen outside our comfort zone. Great thinkers and doers are well-rounded and well-read and take part in a variety of activities. They constantly strive to experience new sources of enlightenment by pushing boundaries, making new connections, and seeing themselves and the world in new ways. Neurobic exercises help motivate us to take risks and step into areas where we have been afraid in order to expand our mind and grow intellectually and emotionally.

Neurobics (*neuron* + *aerobics*) are stretching exercises to increase oxygen and give our brain's neurons more life by experiencing or participating in some new activity, situation, or event. When we stretch our mind, it never returns to its previous shape. Research has indicated that taxing the brain (making it "sweat") with unfamiliar exercises can improve our ability to learn, remember, and solve problems.

For this class, your neurobic exercises must be something you don't ordinarily do and that is appropriate for brain expansion. It could be attending a live performing arts event, beginning an exercise program or playing a new sport, changing your diet or breaking a bad habit, visiting a new place, and so on. Focus on your weakest areas: If your language skills are weak, learn a new word every day; if it's math, put away the calculator. Enter into your neurobic event with an open, clear mind. Allow events to change you. Be willing to grow. Be open to new experiences, and be willing to be changed by them. Learn something new, see new things, respect other people, open yourself, and enrich your life. Get into the world, participate, and enjoy.

Neurobics can do the following:

- Feed great inspiring new information to your brain
- Help you to enjoy and appreciate diversity

---

*Note.* The word *neurobics* was created by James Robert Watson, PhD. Copyright 1988 (www.jamesrobert watson.com/neurobics.html).

- Broaden, stretch, and expand your creative thinking
- Change your life; break out of ruts and grow
- Spice up your life and add some fun
- Encourage you to be an active, alive participant in the world
- Help you to pay attention and not let life just drift by
- Help you to understand someone or something that was a mystery

Sample neurobic activities include the following:

- Walk backward for a day
- Watch no TV for a full week
- Move more (e.g., jogging, walking, hiking)
- Change eating habits
- Quit smoking
- Use your nondominant hand for a day
- Drive into the country and watch the sunrise
- Learn how to play chess
- Solve a crossword puzzle and/or Sudoku each morning
- Practice yoga or meditation
- Start a conversation with one new person every day for a week
- Sample bizarre (to you) foods
- Begin and continue to write in a journal
- Volunteer at a food bank
- Volunteer at a school
- Cover all your mirrors for a week
- Drive a different route to work or school for a week
- Do not access Facebook or any social network for a day
- Eat alone in a restaurant during the lunch or dinner hour
- Do not talk for a day or two
- Take a road trip with no agenda
- Go to a church where you've never been for a weekend service
- Walk the labyrinth on campus

Examples of activities/events to attend include the following:

- Live theater or music performance
- National Cowboy Museum
- Regional museum, science museum, zoo
- Museums and events at other universities

- Cultural festivals
- Arbuckle Wilderness

## Inspiration From Others

Andre Gide

- People cannot discover new lands until they have the courage to lose sight of the shore. (Andre Gide quotes, n.d.)

Anonymous (often attributed to Ralph Waldo Emerson)

- Do not follow where the path may lead. Go instead where there is no path and leave a trail (Do not follow, n.d.).

April Greiman

- I like to step into areas where I am afraid. Fear is a sign that I am going in the right direction. (Lee, 2016)

Eleanor Roosevelt

- Do one thing every day that scares you. (Eleanor Roosevelt quotes, n.d.)

Frank Scully

- Why not go out on a limb? Isn't that where the fruit is? (Frank Scully quotes, n.d.)

John Augustus Shedd

- A ship is safe in a harbor. But a harbor is not what a ship is for. (John Augustus Shedd, 2017).

Jim Watson

- It's all a game. To play is to win. To not play is to lose.
- The simple act of trying raises your chances for success immediately. Not trying guarantees failure.
- Strive to control your mental attitude, your attitude controls your behavior, and your behavior controls your environment.

H. Jackson Brown Jr. (attributed to Mark Twain)

- Twenty years from now, you will be more disappointed by the things that you didn't do than by the ones you did do. (Brown, 1991)

Oprah Winfrey

- You are the single biggest influence in your life. (What I know for sure, n.d.)

Plato

- The life which is unexamined is not worth living. (Baggini, 2005)

Richard Devos

- This is an exciting world. Great moments wait around every corner (The best Richard DeVos quotes, n.d.).

Wayne Gretzky

- You miss 100% of the shots you never take (Brown, 2014).

## Neurobic Activities Project

### *Procedure*

Enjoy the activity or experience (don't worry about taking notes); complete the neurobics report as soon as possible afterward. Submit a report to the drop box by 3:30 p.m. on the due date; see class schedule and D2L. Each will be worth 20 points for a total of 80 points.

### *Specs*

- Use only the form provided.
- Give clear explanations—one page only.
- Proofread for correct spelling and grammar.
- Meet each deadline.
- Each neurobics activity must
    o Have occurred during the week before you turn in the form.
    o Be self-initiated (can't be required for this class or another class).
    o Be significant to you.

## *Evaluation*

Follow the specs and you will earn 20 points per report (80 total). You will lose points for misspelled words or poor grammar, if it was not a truly new or significant experience for you, if you did not initiate the neurobic activity, and if you do not reflect meaningfully on the experience and how it affected you.

## Neurobics Report

Print name:                                    The neurobic event or activity:

Place of event or activity:                    Date(s) of event or activity:

Why does the event or activity qualify as neurobics for you?

How did you grow or change through this experience? Did you see something you can't unsee, learn something you can't unknow, or make some long-term change in behavior?

# Service-Learning Project Rubric

## Service-Learning Project

Each of you will engage in a service-learning project, individually or as part of a group. For the project, you should be engaged in more than "just volunteering." Generally, projects involve a four- to five-hour commitment, but there is great variation. I'll give you some ideas in class, or you can come up with your own idea. You might also contact the Volunteer and Service Learning Center in the Nigh (www.uco.edu/student-affairs/vslc). Project proposals are due by **February 2 at 7:30 p.m.** I'll give you feedback on your proposal based on the following rubric (Table 10B.1) by February 10 at 7:30 p.m.

TABLE 10B.1
**Service-Learning Project Proposal Rubric**

| Criteria | Clearly stated | Unclear | Not there |
|---|---|---|---|
| Description of service-learning project | | | |
| Name and description of agency or group | | | |
| What do you expect to learn? | | | |
| How does the project relate to your life or work? | | | |

Reflection papers (two to three pages, double-spaced, 1-inch margins, 12-point type) are due in by **April 27 at 7:30 p.m.** The paper should address the following about your experience:

1. What was the most useful or meaningful thing you learned?
2. What risks did you take in doing this work, and how did you manage them?
3. Describe one thing you learned about yourself.
4. Describe the ways in which your perspective has changed as a result of this experience.
5. Discuss how this work relates to the material in this class.

**TABLE 10B.2**
**Service-Learning Project Reflection Rubric**

| | Capstone 7 | Milestones 6 | Milestones 5 | Benchmark 4 |
|---|---|---|---|---|
| Meaning | Meaning and usefulness of experience are clearly articulated and insightful. | Meaning and usefulness of experience are articulated and some insights are apparent. | Meaning and usefulness of experience are articulated at a surface level with little insight. | Little or no evidence that student saw meaning or usefulness in the experience. |
| Managing risk | Level of risk is described and student is very clear about how it was managed. | Level of risk is described and some insight is given as to how it was managed. | Level of risk is described and little is said about the way it was managed. | The issue of risk (or not) is barley or not addressed. |
| Learn about self | What student learned about herself or himself is very clearly articulated. | What student learned about herself or himself is well articulated. | What student learned about herself or himself is articulated at a basic level. | Student does not address learning about herself or himself. |
| Change in perspective | Explanation is clear and insightful concerning the specific ways in which the student's perspective has changed. | Explanation is clear concerning the specific ways in which the student's perspective has changed. | Explanation is adequate concerning the specific ways in which the student's perspective has changed. | Student does not explain ways in which her or his perspective has changed or explains poorly. |
| Relate to class | The relationship to class material is clearly articulated. | The relationship to class material is articulated. | The relationship to class material is articulated vaguely. | The relationship to class material is not addressed. |
| Writing mechanics | There are no errors in spelling, grammar, or punctuation. | There are a few errors in spelling, grammar, or punctuation. | There are many errors in spelling, grammar, or punctuation, enough to be distracting. | The errors in spelling, grammar, or punctuation detract seriously from the content. |
| Paper length | Paper is two to three pages. | | | Paper is fewer than two or more than three pages. |

# II

# BELONGING

## Values Affirmation

First-generation students, students from negatively stereotyped groups, and students who grew up in economic insecurity often feel like they don't belong in college and that their input is not needed or even noticed. Recognition that they do have personal values and that those values matter has been shown to have significant positive effects on grades and persistence. Such values-affirming activities are especially effective when they are done at strategic times, such as during transitions (e.g., high school to college), shortly before a major exam, or before a student gives her first speech in a communication class. Values-affirmation interventions, although often lasting for only half an hour or so, have resulted in increased grades in a semester, higher retention to the next semester, and positive feelings of health and well-being up to three years later. G. L. Cohen and Garcia (2014) asserted, "Changing how students think and feel about the classroom can improve their performance and long-term trajectory" (p. 13).

When students in stereotyped groups were asked to choose from a list of values the ones that were most important to them and then to write about why they are important, they attained significantly higher grades than students in a control group over the next two years, resulting in a significant reduction (40%) of the achievement gap between Black and White students (G. L. Cohen, Garcia, Purdie-Vaughns, Apfel, & Brzustoski, 2009).

In two studies with middle school students, Sherman and his colleagues (2013) had groups of students do writing exercises at various intervals that were focused on the values of individual students. In one study, students in the treatment group wrote the exercises four or five times over the period of the study, whereas the control group did not write. The achievement gap, measured by grades, between Latino and White students widened in the control group (as had been the consistent pattern in the past) but not in the experimental group. The positive effects persisted for three years, improving the outlook for these Latino students; the intervention had no effect on the grades of White students. In another study, one group of students wrote daily affirmations, whereas the control group wrote only twice over the school year. As in the first study, the achievement gap for students in the experimental group did not widen, whereas it did for the control group. For the treatment group, the historical downward trend in GPA was eliminated. Sherman and colleagues (2013) explained that the affirmation "prompts students to tell a different story to themselves about their experience and to take a broader view of events in their lives . . . the experience of threat is less likely to set the tone for the rest of their academic tenure" (p. 614).

The effects of these seemingly small interventions have been shown to last up to three years. According to G. L. Cohen, Garcia, Apful, and Master (2006), this is because such interventions can interrupt and potentially reverse what they called the "negative recursive cycle" that occurs when psychological threat, such as stereotype threat, and poor performance act together to create a downward spiral of worsening performance. Interventions such as the values-affirmation writing can stop the cycle and, often, set off a positive recursive cycle when a slight improvement in performance lessens identity threat, freeing up cognitive resources to support future improvements. The results of Cohen and colleagues' (2006) studies have shown that the interventions do interrupt the negative cycle, reversing, for instance, a downward trend in grades. In addition, in their intervention group, an experience of failure did not worsen performance afterward, indicating that the upward cycle was still active in spite of a setback. The researchers pointed out that even if the intervention was small and even if the result is simply minor improvements on several assignments, the cumulative positive effect on the final grade can still be significant.

In addition to the psychological effect of a broadened self-concept and more resiliency in the face of stereotype threat, there is evidence that values-affirmation processes can affect the sympathetic nervous system response to stress. Undergraduate students provided urine samples 14 days before their most stressful exam, to establish a baseline, and on the morning of the exam. Students in the treatment condition wrote two essays on important values during the two weeks preceding the exam, whereas students in a control group did not write. Students in the control condition showed an increase in epinephrine levels, an indicator of sympathetic nervous system activation, from baseline to exam day. Epinephrine levels in the students who had done the affirmation writings did not change from baseline to exam day (Sherman, Bunyan, Creswell, & Jaremka, 2009). Creswell and colleagues (2005) conducted a similar study in a laboratory setting. Participants completed either a values-affirmation task or a control task before encountering a laboratory stress challenge. Compared with the control group, those who had completed the values-affirmation task had significantly lower cortisol responses to stress.

Figure 11.1 is the list of values and instructions I use when I do the affirmation exercise in my classes and in other settings with students. I want students to write about how their top values have influenced their life and choices so the values seem real in a concrete way. Of course, the specifics of the instructions and the list of values can be revised to fit the situation. When I first put together the list, I started with lists that I found on the Internet and distributed a draft list to 10 or so of my colleagues. I asked them to add or subtract any items to fit the context of our university and community; I incorporated their suggestions, resulting in the list for the exercise shown in Figure 11.1.

**Figure 11.1.** Personal values affirmation exercise.

| | | | |
|---|---|---|---|
| Wisdom | Reliability | Integrity | Enthusiasm |
| Winning | Productivity | Inspiration | Efficiency |
| Well-being | Power | Initiative | Dignity |
| Wealth | Personal growth | Independence | Dependence |
| Volunteering | Perseverance | Humor | Curiosity |
| Truth | Peace | Humility | Creativity |
| Trust | Patriotism | Hope | Courtesy |
| Tradition | Patience | Honesty | Courage |
| Teamwork | Orderliness | Heritage | Cooperation |
| Success | Optimism | Health | Conflict resolution |
| Spirituality | Openness | Harmony | Confidence |
| Simplicity | Open communication | Generosity | Competitiveness |
| Service | Nature | Fun | Competence |
| Self-reliance | Mercy | Friendship | Compassion |
| Self-esteem | Making a difference | Freedom | Community |
| Self-discipline | Loyalty | Forgiveness | Commitment |
| Safety | Love | Flexibility | Collaboration |
| Sacrifice | Listening | Fitness | Civility |
| Romance | Learning | Financial stability | Caring |
| Risk-taking | Leadership | Family | Boldness |
| Responsibility | Kindness | Fame | Beauty |
| Respect | Justice | Faith | Ambition |
| Resilience | Joy | Fairness | Adaptability |
| Reputation | Job security | Excellence | Achievement |
| Religion | Intuition | Ethical behavior | Accountability |

*(Continues)*

**Figure 11.1.** (*Continued*)

1. From the list, circle the 10 values that you consider to be the most important in your life.
2. Think for a bit about each of those 10 values. Put a second circle around the 3 that are the most important of all of them.
3. Write a letter explaining to another student in your class why these values are important to you and what difference they have made in your life. Give some examples of things you have done or choices you have made in your life based on these 3 values.


Although this affirmation exercise is fairly straightforward, a few cautions are in order. The list of values needs to include those to which students can relate. A good practice is to instruct students during the intervention that if there is something that they value that's not on the list, then they may add it. The point is to affirm each student's perspective, so the specific list of values is not material to the exercise. The person doing the exercise must be sincere; if not, students will realize it. For example, an instructor who has shown hostility to students in a certain group who then asks them to write about their values may be seen as insincere, and students might not take the exercise seriously. If the exercise is done in an effort to remedy a negative situation in a class or group, it might be a good idea to have an outside person work through it with the students. In addition, Yeager and Walton (2011) suggested that a values-affirmation exercise given by an instructor who has been told to do it, with little understanding or commitment to the purpose, could become a farce, possibly doing more harm than good.

## Connecting the Known to the Unknown

There may be many reasons to explain the powerful effect of asking students to write about their values. One might be acknowledging that all students bring something valuable to the learning environment. Both Gonzales, Moll, and Amanti (1995) and Glisczinski (2011) told us that students learn better when their own experiences are linked to what goes on in the classroom. When we have students who come from disadvantaged educational environments or who grew up in economic insecurity, we often focus on their deficits, what they *don't* bring to the classroom. Sugarman (2010) suggested that we reframe our view of these students and try to see their strengths. She cited the explanation from Gonzales and colleagues (1995) to describe what educators call *funds of knowledge*:

The understanding that students, families, and communities are comprised not only of struggles, but also of strength. In other words, students and families possess funds of knowledge, or bodies of knowledge and skills derived from household and community life, that when incorporated into the classroom may support and enhance students' educational experiences. (Sugarman, 2010, p. 97)

Glisczinski (2011), in mapping how learning happens, related what Medina (2008) told us, that our "brains favor and retain the lessons learned through concrete experiences with emotionally cogent and relevant stimuli" (para. 1). That means the subject needs to be connected somehow to past experience and that there has to be meaning to the connection. When we start with students' funds of knowledge, their brains will light up, as Glisczincki (2011) said, and grow in response to the stimuli of new information. When students give Life Reports (described on p. 86 in "Pecha Kucha Life Reports"), they learn about themselves and others through "emotionally cogent" content. Another way that I connect experience and students' funds of knowledge with sociology course content is in the discussion questions from the reading for which students come prepared every week. The following is from my syllabus:

For each class session, read the assigned chapter and come prepared with one or more of the following:

- An example from your life or from the life of someone you know that illustrates a concept (or the opposite) from the reading.
- Questions you have about something in the reading that you'd like to have addressed by the class.
- Something from news or other media that relates to the reading.
- Sharing of a book, article, film, experience, etc. that might help others in the class understand a concept in the reading.
- Related to the readings, something that you don't yet understand or that you need help with and about which others in the class might have some wisdom to share with you.

Because the students represent diversity in age, gender, race/ethnicity, life experience, and socioeconomic status, the variety of the offerings enriches the entire class. More importantly, students feel that their ideas and their views about what they're reading are valued and contribute positively to the learning of everyone in the class. (There is time for only a few people to actually share their question or example during a class meeting—I draw their names randomly each session—but I collect their notes and read them, following up in the next class on student questions or insights that I want to share with the class.)

G. L. Cohen and Garcia (2014) cited a study by Hulleman and Harackiewicz (2009) in which high school science students were encouraged to connect what they were learning to their everyday life. In this way, students saw the content as personally relevant, not something academic and removed. The intervention resulted in higher grades for students for whom there had been low expectations for success.

When we see students' values and life experiences as funds of knowledge that contribute to their learning, we affirm each of the students, and by connecting new material to what they already know, we cooperate with the way their brain prefers to function. In this way, we increase the likelihood that students will feel a sense of belonging and that their learning will be enhanced. J. Carlson (2015–2016) described the ideal interaction with students as whole beings in the following:

> So as a teacher, I'm not just teaching "the material." I'm teaching "the students," which means that I'm inviting them, each of them, with their particular present blends of connectedness to past realities, to interact with the "stuff" of our course and with each other. (p. 61)

Given that the system of public primary and secondary education in the United States operates in the same sociocultural environment as does higher education, many students arrive at college unprepared academically for college work. No amount of psychological or social intervention can create knowledge and skill that is not there. However, with a growth mind-set, persistence, and our help and support, students can build on their nonacademic funds of knowledge to catch up on the basics. Once they have built their self-efficacy from small learning achievements, they can apply those funds of knowledge to college-level work.

Yeager and Walton (2011) cautioned that seemingly valid interventions can be derailed when they are delivered in such a way that a different message reaches the students. They referenced the Hulleman and Harackiewicz (2009) study about high school science students who had low expectations for success. Those students' grades improved when they generated and wrote about ways in which the lessons were relevant to their life. When the instructor *told* students why the lessons were important, the intervention actually had a negative effect on grades for low-expectation students.

## Identification With Academic Self

In light of the values-affirmation exercises and thinking back to the discussion of disidentification with academics, we can now effectively use these concepts to support students in taking on academic success as part of their self-concept. If a Black male student chooses, for instance, *competitive, loyal,* and *reliable* as his top values and then writes an essay in which he describes his reasoning, those values are affirmed in this new, academic setting. Maybe he will begin adding academics as a domain in which his self-concept could survive and even flourish. Other interventions might also help students add an academic aspect to their existing self-concept.

It's not exactly an intervention like the others, but having the faculty of an institution more closely reflect the racial/ethnic population of students could contribute to students' ability to see themselves as "college material." One of the downsides of the racial mismatch between students and teachers is that non-Black teachers may have much lower expectations of Black students than do Black teachers (Gershenson, 2015). Analyzing data from a national study of U.S. 10th graders, Gershenson (2015) found significant differences in teachers' estimates of whether a student would, in the future, earn a four-year college degree. In the case of Black students, non-Black teachers were about 30% less likely to predict college graduation than were Black teachers. We know that students are very sensitive to teachers' expectations and that low expectations can result in a self-fulfilling prophecy of actual low performance. Instructors must communicate high expectations of all students and offer them the support they need to meet them.

Steele (1997) emphasized the importance of "potential-affirming adult relationships" (p. 624). This relates back to Dweck's "not yet" feedback. G. L. Cohen, Steele, and Ross (1999) found that Black students were strongly motivated by critical feedback when it was given with messages of optimism about the students' potential. Some researchers have pointed out the potential damage of placing students in remedial classes, as they can be perceived through the "lens of an ability-demeaning stereotype" (Steele, 1997, p. 625), whereas high academic challenge conveys respect for students' potential to learn. Remedial placement can, by increasing stereotype threat, undermine performance, thus causing the opposite of the intended effect.

Oyserman, Bybee, and Terry (2006) took on the task of helping eighth-grade low-income Black (72% of group), Hispanic (17%), and White (11%) students imagine their future self as academically successful. In 10 workshop sessions, students completed exercises to bring out the funds of knowledge each of them would be taking to high school with them, to make their future academic self seem more attainable, and to see that "difficulties are normative and not self-defining" (p. 191). Two years later, these students, compared to those in the control group, had higher grades, better attendance, less disruptive behavior, less depression, and were less likely to have repeated eighth grade. A Black male college senior said in an interview (study described in chapter 12), "Being smart was not cool in high school. People want to be cool. I suppressed my gifted and talented mentality." He had not developed what Oyserman, Bybee, and Terry (2006) called his "academic possible self" (p. 189); maybe he couldn't imagine himself as a successful student *and* a young man with a strong Black identity.

This next bit could as easily fit under growth mind-set, but I put it here because it seems relevant to helping students shift their expectations of themselves and to encourage self-identification based on academic ability. Yeager and colleagues (2014) worked with seventh graders from a middle-class, racially diverse middle school. They asked each student to write an essay about a personal hero, and the teachers marked the essays, typically with feedback such as "unclear," "give examples," and "wrong word." Then they randomly attached one of two sticky notes to each essay. Half the students received a bland message such as "I'm giving you these comments so that you'll have feedback on your paper." For the other half of the students, the note said, "I'm giving you these comments because I have very high expectations and I know you can reach them." The teachers then gave the students an opportunity to revise their essay. Eighty-seven percent of White students who received the encouraging message turned in revised essays, compared to 62% who got the bland note. Among Black students, the rates were 72% compared to 17%, a much greater effect. Yeager and colleagues (2014) concluded that the Black students were more motivated to try to improve their work when the teacher both reminded them of high performance expectations and assured them that the teacher believed the students could meet the high standards. I suspect that these students, most of whom decided to revise their essay, at least in this situation, felt the message that it was safe to connect with their academic self.

## Pecha Kucha Life Reports

In classes at first-year and senior/graduate levels, I ask students to give a Life Report. They use a presentation style called Pecha Kucha (Klein Dytham Architecture, 2003), in which they create 20 PowerPoint slides (primarily pictures), and each slide is shown for 20 seconds. I started using this presentation method because it's a way to share an idea or tell a story that's not completely focused on the written word and, thus, respects cultural norms that value the spoken word. Students in my senior/graduate sociology course (human behavior over the lifespan) share with the class a brief story of their life in which they tell about the circumstances of their birth, their parents and siblings, where they lived and went to school, and positive and negative milestones. As a way to introduce myself, I give my own Life Report on the first day of class, demonstrating the presentation method and, more importantly, role-modeling openness about my life and willingness to take risk. Students discover that some of their classmates have very different backgrounds than they do, and in the process, everyone's experiences are affirmed and respected. The students show great empathy toward one another and realize that, in spite of their backgrounds, they are all now together in this class with the same goal of getting a college education.

For first-year students, the Life Report can be focused on a brief reflection of family and high school, plans for college major, and plans and hopes for career and life after college. The process helps students with the development (or creation) of their self-identification as college students. They can see that some students come from relative privilege and others from relative disadvantage but that they are all together in this classroom at this moment, all with the potential of belonging. As in the other class, if the instructor gives her own Life Report, students get a sense of safety and are encouraged to be open and honest.

During the last several semesters, I asked students to reflect on what they learned from the Life Report process, both giving and listening. The major themes and some illustrative responses are shown in Table 11.1.

## Relationship-Building in Classes

In 1972, Donald Bligh wrote a comprehensive book about teaching in higher education called *What's the Use of Lectures?* in which he suggested strongly that an instructor who only lectures is using a teaching method that, by itself, is a very ineffective way for students to learn. We have known for several decades that lecture alone is not ideal, especially for getting students to think critically or to change perspectives. But, apparently, it is a method still in frequent use. D. J. Smith and Valentine (2012) looked at the practices of 744 instructors at 8 technical colleges and found that almost all of them (93%) reported lecturing for more than half of the class sessions, and 53% reported lecturing in all of the sessions. A study by S. Freeman and colleagues (2014) in the STEM (science, technology, engineering, and mathematics) disciplines showed that students in lecture-only classes were 1.5 times more likely to fail than students in classes where active learning strategies were used. They found that in classes in which students were active participants instead of passive learners, failure rates were reduced, and scores on exams increased by almost half a standard deviation.

**TABLE 11.1**

**Learning From Life Reports in Two Classes**

| Themes | Student Statements |
|---|---|
| **Success Central (First-Year Experience Class), _n_ = 25** | |
| Classmates, differences, and commonalities | • Some people have had things happen in their lives that have also happened in my life.<br>• So many of us came from different backgrounds, yet we're so similar and all ended up at the same university, in the same class.<br>• I've learned that each of us is here to contribute something important to the world.<br>• Really never judge a book by its cover—we all have so many layers.<br>• I learned about some of the hardships that many of my classmates have faced. I also learned a lot about their background and families. |
| Insights about self | • I learned that where you come from and where you've been can shape who you are, but it doesn't have to.<br>• It seemed to make it more concrete for myself why I am here and what I am working toward and goals that I definitely plan on achieving before I die.<br>• I had to really think about what I want in my future, which I've never thought about too deeply.<br>• People do care what I have to say.<br>• I realized how much I have accomplished in high school, how much my friends and family have impacted my life, and my drive toward my life goals.<br>• It makes me and my classmates closer when we share important stuff about ourselves. |
| Self-concept as college student | • Everyone is starting out at the bottom, and everyone is struggling to make friends, find certain places, and people are scared to ask questions. This understanding helped me because I know not to be scared about things.<br>• As much as I love my friends and enjoy spending time with them, I can survive and thrive on my own.<br>• High school was too easy. I need to study harder in college.<br>• It helped me to better understand that all of these people in my class are freshmen just like me, and that they are new here and working toward a career as well. |

|  | • Everyone is from a different background. Learn to make new friends and learn about them and their life and drive because it will help me grow as an individual.
• Everything that has happened in my life has gotten me where I am, so I'm glad everything happened.
• I need to take advantage of the position I'm in and work to the best of my ability every day. |
|---|---|
| **Human Behavior and the Social Environment, $n = 59$** | |
| Different backgrounds but all fundamentally the same | • All of my classmates have hopes, dreams, failures, disappointments, and successes in their lives.
• There is something empowering about verbally owning your life's events. It kinda kills the shame.
• I learned how diverse a classroom can be. People have experienced very different lives yet we all ended up in the same classroom.
• Family comes in many forms.
• The huge disparity between students on campus. Some students come from families who could give them anything. They are so humble when you meet them.
• In the classroom we are equal.
• As distant as I sometimes feel from other's actual experiences, the emotions and empathy we share makes [sic] us a lot more similar than we are different.
• How we handle a situation has almost everything to do with what happens next.
• People's stories are important, and I believe it's good to let each person have the authority to say it for herself or himself
• The most important thing that I thought was useful in life is that all of us have problems and that it is not just me.
• This was crucial for me to understand, which made me feel not alone in my quest for being a better human being.
• Knowing that each of us is human and has problems is what unites us all.
• I realized the struggles in my family are universal and that made me feel less alone. |
| Insights about self | • My view of the world is very much through my lens based on my own life experience.
• I am proud of myself. It wasn't easy getting here, and I should give myself credit for doing the best I can despite everything telling me to give up.
• I should thank my parents more. |

*(Continues)*

**TABLE 11.1** (*Continued*)

| Themes | Student Statements |
|---|---|
| Insights about self | <ul><li>After walking through everything that has happened in my life—even the minor things—and then laying out my goals in what I want to accomplish next, I am encouraged to work hard to achieve those goals.</li><li>I realized how young I am, and it's okay to not have it all together.</li><li>I know I continue to grow through my life experiences and learn every day something from those around me.</li><li>My adversities have been what have made me and influenced who I will become after college.</li><li>People come from all walks of life, and it does not matter where you come from, only where you end up.</li><li>No matter what, I can learn from my past and make better decisions in the future.</li></ul> |
| We're resilient | <ul><li>Each person in our class has experienced great adversity and come through it stronger.</li><li>Many classmates had a very rough life and some big obstacles to get to where they are now.</li><li>People, given time and a little help, can overcome major setbacks.</li><li>No matter the %^\$@ I had been through, my pain was not without growth.</li><li>Listening to my classmates' life reports makes me realize that I am sitting around strong people.</li></ul> |
| Don't judge a book by its cover | <ul><li>People contain so much more substance than I could ever imagine just from looking at them.</li><li>All of us (my classmates and all humans) have universal themes that connect our lives (i.e., we all have families or long to have families, we all crave a sense of belonging, we all want to be successful, and we all share a uniquely human experience).</li><li>Not one of us is alike, and therefore we should not compare ourselves. No family is completely normal.</li><li>I also learned that everyone has stories you don't know about so don't be so quick to judge.</li><li>Every person is doing their best, no matter the circumstances.</li><li>It helps me with my career by looking at the whole picture of a person and not just their problem.</li><li>I need to learn to understand people's history and story before I jump to conclusions.</li><li>People are not what they appear to be on the outside. We all have a unique, deep, and rich experience that makes us who we are.</li><li>I learned that people may look good and happy on the outside but may be going through adversity both personally and in their families.</li></ul> |

Even given the evidence that lectures do not produce desirable student learning, there is another reason that lecture alone is not a helpful teaching strategy, especially in the first year and especially for nonmajority and first-generation students. If the instructor is just talking to a group of students, no relationships are being formed. If the lecturer has an engaging speaking style and presents interesting information, individual students might feel a relationship with the instructor, but the instructor may or may not feel a reciprocal relationship. More important, however, if all that happens in a class period is that the instructor lectures and the students listen and take notes, no relationships are being formed between and among students in the class. For students, it's an experience of what early-learning educators call *parallel play*. This is when, at around two years old, children are in the same space and playing, but they're not playing with each other; there's no interaction and no relationship. College students may come to the same lecture twice a week for 15 weeks, and even though they are "sharing" the same experience, no relationships are formed. The classroom may look like the one shown in Figure 11.2, with the possibility of a relationship between individual students and the instructor but little chance for connections between students.

Given that a sense of belonging seems to be a critical factor in student success, it makes sense to use the opportunity in every class to connect students with each other. There are many methods to accomplish this, such as

**Figure 11.2.** Student relates to lecturer only.

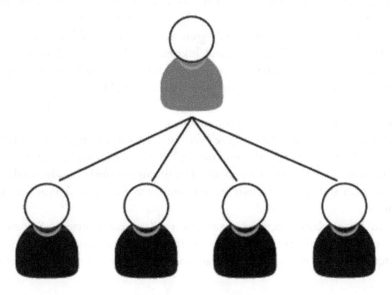

having students work out a problem as a group, "teach" each other a concept, take quizzes in groups, and exchange ideas in pairs or triads. In large class sections, facilitating this kind of interactive learning environment often results in an enhanced relationship between students and instructor as well. Hoffman, Richmond, Morrow, and Salomone (2002), in a study of first-year college students found that a

> "sense of belonging" to the institution stems from perceptions of "valued involvement" in the collegiate environment. . . . This perception of "valued involvement" appears predicated on: 1) establishing functionally supportive peer relationships—"functional," in terms of the ability of the relationship(s) to directly aid students in meeting the challenges and changes of their new environment; and 2) the belief that faculty are compassionate and that the student is more than just another face in the crowd. (pp. 249, 251)

From surveys of 238 university first-year students, T. M. Freeman, Anderman, and Jensen (2007) found that certain instructor actions and characteristics were associated with students' sense of belonging. The most important was encouraging student participation and interaction. This, along with instructor warmth and organization, was associated with student motivation and achievement.

First-year general education classes could be excellent settings in which to help students get connected to other students and form relationships with faculty. In my classes, I encourage students to appreciate both the diversity among them and the ways in which they have shared experiences. In sociology, I have students stand in groups in different parts of the room based on the size of the town where they grew up, how many siblings they have, whether they have children or grandchildren, or whether they have traveled outside of the United States. Then we divide into groups of five with the goal of maximizing diversity. Those are the groups they will be in for the semester. I distribute papers on which they record their names, e-mail addresses, and phone numbers; they make six copies, one for each of them and one for me. Each class period, they take a quiz over the assigned reading, first individually and then as a group; the scores on the individual quiz and the group quiz contribute equally to the final grade. The group members are the students' contacts for the class and often become important support systems for each other.

In large lecture sections, especially in first-year courses, an instructor could form students into triads on the first day and have the students exchange contact information. If that triad talked together even once during a class session about course content, relationships would begin to form. Students might begin to be accountable to one another—someone would notice if one of the three were not in class. This could make a significant difference for a beginning student—the fact that someone cared if he or she showed up. If a student had five classes and formed the beginnings of a relationship with two people in each, she would have 10 students she could contact if she felt the need. We know that active learning techniques increase learning, and they can also create situations in which students could feel a sense of belonging by forging new relationships with fellow students and the instructor, therefore increasing the likelihood of persistence.

## Helping Relationships: Mattering

Straumanis (2012) advocated that instructors provide plenty of social interaction and the use of active learning approaches to ensure engagement. She suggested that the following techniques are much better than passive listening and are best used alternately or in combination:

- short writing breaks during lectures, labs, or other activities;
- peer explanation and self-explanation (requiring *all* learners to repeat what they have learned in their own words);
- discussion or problem solving with others in teams or pairs ("buddy system"); [and]
- "guided inquiry"—structured lesson delivery in which the material to be learned is divided into graduated increments and presented by means of carefully designed problems to be solved collectively by small groups of students. (p. 10)

Eric Mazur, a Harvard physics professor and a strong advocate and model of teaching to help students learn, has found that peer instruction is often a more effective way for students to learn a new concept than a lecture about it. In an interview (Lambert, 2012), he explained how it works:

Here's what happened. . . . First, when one student has the right answer and the other doesn't, the first one is more likely to convince the second— it's hard to talk someone into the wrong answer when they have the right one. More important, a fellow student is *more likely* to reach them than Professor Mazur—and this is the crux of the method. You're a student and you've only recently learned this, so you still know where you got hung up, because it's not that long ago that *you* were hung up on that very same thing. Whereas Professor Mazur got hung up on this point when he was

17, and he no longer remembers how difficult it was back then. He has lost the ability to understand what a beginning learner faces. (para. 7)

Mazur has observed that this kind of instruction has tripled students' gains in knowledge and eliminated the gender gap between male and female undergraduates. Both males and females gain, but females gain disproportionally more, and the gap closes.

Within groups that are intentionally formed to maximize diversity, everyone has something about which he or she is an expert; everyone brings something to the table. With guidance, students see that diversity of knowledge, background, and perspective is a strength in a group learning situation.

Outside of the classroom, students can be trained as peer advisers and, for reasons much like those given by Mazur for the success of peers in explaining physics concepts, can introduce first-year students to what they really need to know to succeed. As pointed out by Heidi Koring (2005) at NACADA (The Global Community for Academic Advising), students advise students every day, in the library, on the bus, in the Union, in the pub, and elsewhere: "Formal peer advising programs direct and channel peer advising to ensure that students are given advice by peers trained to impart accurate information and to make appropriate referrals" (para. 1). According to Koring,

> Peer advising offers several advantages, including versatility, compatibility with pre-existing academic advising programs, sensitivity to student needs, and the ability to extend the range and scope of advising to times and venues when advising is not usually available. Additionally, those serving as peer advisors benefit from the leadership development included in such programs. (para. 3)

At American University, peer advisers offered socioemotional support and information about support services by providing a friendly ear for the expression of concerns and requests for help. The first outreach was through e-mail, and researchers found that when the adviser was a male, male students were 26.5 percentage points more likely to engage with the adviser than if the adviser was female (Ellis & Gershenson, 2016). At American University, the majority of students are female, so that might explain why male students might want to connect with another male. This finding reminds us to pay attention to identity contingencies that might affect a student's comfort with a peer adviser.

Duke University gives this explanation about its peer advising program:

> Each year, experienced students volunteer to serve as peer advisors to first-
> and second-year students, offering the perspective of someone who has
> been where you are now. Peer advisors can share with you how they formed
> meaningful mentoring relationships with faculty, assist you in navigating
> online registration and help you learn to distinguish what is merely popular
> from what is individually meaningful to you. (advising.duke.edu/peer)

This description highlights one of the strongest assets of a peer adviser, which
is that he has, very recently, been in the shoes of a first-year student. He can
still remember what it was like to be new on campus and the questions that
he wished someone would have answered for him. With training, peer advisers can combine their empathy and natural connectedness to an age-mate
with accurate information about resources on campus to lend beginning students the support they need and, it is hoped, also help them feel that essential
sense of belonging.

## Academic and Social Counter-Spaces

In 1997, Beverly Tatum wrote the book *"Why Are All the Black Kids Sitting Together in the Cafeteria?" and Other Conversations About Race.* With
the title, she was making the point that the reason we don't know why the
Black kids are sitting together is that we can't even ask the question. When
I recently read about academic and social counter-spaces, I immediately
thought of the kids in the cafeteria. They, along with groups of Hispanic
students, Asian students, Native American students, skateboarders, gamers,
and others, were trying to establish what Solórzano, Ceja, and Yosso (2000)
called "counter-spaces," places where they can feel safe and relax in their
own skin.

In their study of racial climate on college campuses, Solórzano and colleagues (2000) held focus groups with 38 Black male and female students
who were attending three elite, predominantly White, Research I institutions:

> In response to the daily barrage of racial microaggressions that they endure
> both in and outside of their classes . . . students . . . indicated that they
> are creating academic and social "counter-spaces" on and off their cam-
> puses. These counter-spaces serve as sites where deficit notions of people of

color can be challenged and where a positive collegiate racial climate can be established. (p. 70)

Māori are the indigenous people of New Zealand, and as a result of colonization and loss of traditional lands and livelihoods, they are disproportionately poorer, less educated, sicker, and underemployed compared to White New Zealanders. Pasifika students, who come from or whose ancestors came from islands in the South Pacific—Sāmoa, Cook Islands, Tonga, Niue, Fiji, Tokelau, and Tuvalu—share many of the negative health and social indicators with Māori (Marriott & Sim, 2014). At Victoria University in Wellington (VUW), New Zealand, I visited the *Te Herenga Waka Marae*, a traditional Māori cultural center where students and staff can welcome visitors and gather for academic and social occasions. In the Māori culture, a *marae* is the center of the community, a meeting place for ceremonies and social gatherings. The VUW *marae* is both a gathering space and a teaching space, a safe place where Māori students can come for lunch and to study. Students are involved in the *marae* in many ways, including cooking, cleaning, and participating in various ritual activities.

Writing about the VUW *marae* and others at New Zealand colleges and universities, Adds, Hall, Higgins, and Higgins (2011) stated, "Often they inspire a personal and emotive learning experience, with students studying the Māori language, culture and identity in ways that extend beyond vocational training to learning for self-discovery" (p. 541). As a setting where students can recover bandwidth, Adds and his colleagues related a statement about the "role that *marae* play in providing a space for Māori student to 'rejuvenate their souls, to reaffirm their identity . . . to network as Māori in a pan-tribal context and so support each other in their studies' (Ka'ai, 2008, p. 194)" (p. 545). There is also an area for Pasifika students at VUW where they can study, individually or in groups, where they feel safe and nurtured. These are intentional counter-spaces created by the institution as part of its commitment to the success of Māori and Pasifika students.

At San Jose State University, facing persistently low graduation rates, Pizarro and his colleagues called hundreds of students who had dropped out to ask them why they left the university. The students identified some institutional barriers and said that they never felt like they were part of the campus community. Pizarro decided that they needed to give students a sense of community so they would be better able to weather the inevitable crises that happen to students who are balancing school, work, family, and, for many, cultural values that sometimes run counter to their educational goals. He started having activities to engage students and families, such as Pozole Night in the Student Union, where they serve traditional Mexican soup, and students study, meet with tutors, and talk with counselors and other professionals. Similar culture-relevant events are held for Black students as well. The hope is that these will become effective counter-spaces where students can feel safe and comfortable, where they can get back a bit of their mental bandwidth that is depleted by daily pressures (Emanuel, 2016).

The Office of Diversity and Inclusion (ODI) at the University of Central Oklahoma is a small space on the main floor of the university center that houses three staff members and a couple of student workers. At most times during the week, you'll find many students of color; lesbian, gay, bisexual, and transgender students and their allies; and various other students who have come to this counter-space, knowing they'll be welcomed and accepted for who they are. This is an evolved counter-space, not designed for a gathering place, but the students have made it one anyway.

The spaces mentioned here are examples of ones at least partially set up by the institution, sometimes, as in the case of ODI, redefined a bit by students in a way not expected by staff. Other counter-spaces just evolve, such as when a study group for a class morphs into a social support group that lasts beyond the semester. For students of color at predominantly White institutions, spaces where they can get educational, emotional, and cultural support are necessary. Solórzano and colleagues (2000) found that counter-spaces were critical for Black students as a way to help inoculate them against the adverse effects of racism:

> Marginalized students are often familiar with the groups' voices being silenced in the classroom discourse or with having their personal and/or group experiences and beliefs discounted. These negative experiences occur in addition to the pervasiveness of the cultural-deficit discourse in the academy (Valencia & Solórzano, 1997). Perhaps as a response to their position of marginality on their campuses, the students in our study seemed to create academic and social counter-spaces along racial or gender lines. Nonetheless, in separating themselves from racially or gender-uncomfortable situations, this group of African American college students appeared to be utilizing their counter-spaces on their own terms. This confirms that the creation of such counter-spaces is an important strategy for minority students' academic survival (Solórzano & Villalpando, 1998). (p. 71)

When students create their own counter-spaces, we are sometimes lucky as faculty and professional staff when students choose a place near us and invite us to be part of it. We can, in our institutions, make sure that there are spaces where students can "hang out" in safety and peace. Especially on campuses where most of the students are commuters, thought should be given to providing "setting down" spaces where students can relax for a few minutes and feel that they're part of the community even though they come and go and have many other demands on their time and attention. These students, especially, need a safe space to take a deep breath and gather a bit of mental bandwidth as they transition from their work and family to their academic life.

# 12

# DECREASING STEREOTYPE THREAT AND IDENTITY THREAT

S tereotype threat and identity threat take up critical mental bandwidth
that is then unavailable for learning. Steele (2010) contended that
reducing these threats is just as important as instruction in knowledge
and skills:

> No amount of instruction, no matter how good it is, can reduce these
> deficits if it doesn't also keep identity threat low. Without that, threat will
> always have the first claim on students' attention and mental resources. So
> neither approach—providing instructional opportunities or reducing iden-
> tity threat—is sufficient, by itself, to improve academic performance, espe-
> cially for ability-stereotyped students. Both are necessary. (pp. 181–182)

Picking back up on the growth mind-set theme, Goff, Steele, and Davies
(2008) conducted a project in which they were looking for a mind-set that
would facilitate conversations between White people and people of color
about a difficult topic: racial profiling. White students, under this circum-
stance of discussing a race-loaded topic, suffered identity threat, worrying
that students of color would perceive them as racist if they said the wrong
thing. The researchers experimented with various messages to the White
students, such as assuring them that they wouldn't be judged by what they
said or that differences of opinion were natural and appreciated. Only when
researchers told students to view the conversation as a learning experience
did the students seem to be able to shed the identity threat and be willing
to enter into the conversation. "With a learning goal, mistakes become just
mistakes, not signs of immutable racism" (Steele, 2010, p. 208). When people share learning as a goal, trust is built and missteps become less significant.

Growth mind-set, then, can help reduce identity threat and free up cognitive resources for learning.

Reducing identity threat is addressed further in chapter 13 in a discussion of institutional structures and processes, specifically critical mass and public images. Here, I discuss two strategies to decrease the power of stereotype threat for students in certain nonmajority groups.

## Nonpejorative Attribution

To break the cycle of poor performance and anxiety that leads to more poor performance, T. D. Wilson and Linville (1985) thought that it would help if students could shift the attribution for poor performance from pejorative (the student's lack of intelligence) to nonpejorative (the context). This shift moves the location of the problem from the individual to the social circumstances of being a student in certain nonmajority groups. Even a small shift in students' views in this area can have very positive effects on academic performance. J. Aronson and colleagues (1999) suggested that stereotype threat is a common phenomenon that affects nonmajority students: "It is a predicament that stems from quite normal responses to the low or demeaning expectations that come to the individual in the form of cultural stereotypes" (p. 44).

T. D. Wilson and Linville (1985) convinced entering college students that early difficulties were attributable not to stable internal causes (fixed intelligence) but to temporary external causes (the transition from high school to college). As a result, students improved their grades in the second year and were more likely to stay in college than were nonintervention students. Walton and Cohen (2007) found that outcomes of first-year students improved when they were presented with data from junior and senior students from all ethnic groups who reported that as first-year students, they also had worried about whether they would be accepted and that the worry decreased over time. In a later study, Walton and Cohen (2011) found that students who had been told about the experiences of students before them, over a three-year period, had increased GPAs and cut the minority achievement gap by half. In addition, students' self-reported health and well-being improved, and visits to the doctor decreased. The intervention had no effect on the grades of White students.

Instead of passively presenting first-year students with data from senior students, first-year students could be more engaged by interviewing senior students themselves, who were matched with them by various demographic characteristics, about their experience as first-year students. Over time, this collection of data from these successful students could be used in interventions with new students who might arrive at college having experienced stereotype threat in their education and life and might feel significant *belongingness uncertainty*. The assurance that students like them have gone on to be successful will likely add to their sense of belonging. In the group of Black students in the Walton and Cohen (2007) study, normalizing doubts about social belonging and presenting them as temporary was associated with the students' sense of belonging being less dependent on the quality of their day, increased engagement in achievement behaviors (e.g., studying), and improvements in their GPAs.

At the University of Central Oklahoma, we began a focused program to support Black male first-year students, as this group has the lowest persistence and graduation rate of all our students. In this program, called the Black Male Initiative (BMI), Black male first-year students are invited to engage in a common orientation class; meet with sophomore, junior, and senior mentors; receive a small financial incentive toward tuition after initial success; meet in Brotherhood Circles; and have the option to take a common African American history course during the second semester of their first year. With two colleagues from that program, I started a research project in which we interviewed Black male seniors or recent graduates about their experiences as first-year students. We will share the results with students in the BMI, hoping to help them understand that struggles are common and that students who have come before them have overcome the challenges and have achieved academic success. We have interviewed 13 men to date; see Table 12.1 for some of the major themes and exemplary statements.

Stereotype threat can be lessened if we can make race less important to students as they interpret their experiences on campus. Steele and his colleagues at Michigan State (Steele, 2010) sponsored late-night bull sessions for students in groups of up to 15 in which they discussed personally relevant issues. Students talked about topics such as family and parents, friendship and romantic relationships, and what was going on in their classes. Consistent with the demographics of Michigan State, there were usually no more than 3 Black students in any group, but participation made the most difference to these students, who got one-third of a letter grade higher than Black students in a control group. Steele (2010) reasoned that the Black students in these discussion sessions learned that the struggles students have in college are very common across race.

> This fact changes black students' narrative; it makes racial identity less central to interpreting experience and increases trust in the university environment. Having a narrative that requires less vigilance leaves more mental energy and motivation available for academic work and thus improved the grades of the black students in the program. (p. 167)

**TABLE 12.1**

**Black Male Seniors and Graduates Recalling Their First Year of College**

| Themes | Student Statements |
|---|---|
| Personal choices or attributes | • Hardest part was coming to class. I liked to hang out with friends who were not in college.<br>• Introvert—hard to get out of my shell.<br>• Strong schedule—study, work, relax—so no time to get into trouble.<br>• Didn't know resources and didn't care.<br>• Didn't see positivity in my life.<br>• Independent—wouldn't ask for help.<br>• Wasn't surrounded by positive people.<br>• First year, so much was thrown at me, it was overwhelming. I just took a step back.<br>• Living on campus, I was more focused. |
| Family | • Parents pushed going to college.<br>• I didn't want to disappoint my parents.<br>• Mom says, "The energy you put out in the world you get back."<br>• I was afraid of going back home as a failure.<br>• Parents gave me discipline.<br>• When living at home, family came first [distraction from school]. |
| Institutional factors | • Teacher told us to network, create a positive environment.<br>• Didn't understand and the teacher thought I should—I didn't feel confident and didn't have the autonomy to figure it out.<br>• College wasn't as hard as I expected. I wish it would have been harder; I would have taken it more seriously.<br>• I had a math instructor who was bent on students succeeding. Emphasized willingness to help. |
| Money | • Had no money, needed to get a campus job—hard to focus with money worries.<br>• It is a lot easier when you don't worry about money.<br>• College and books are expensive.<br>• Parents didn't have money to give me.<br>• Sent most of refund check [financial aid] to Mom [single parent].<br>• Worked 30 hours a week at an overnight shift at a hotel and then went to school during the day. |
| Advice for new students | • Build a team of positive support/make connections.<br>• Get involved/take risks.<br>• Have self-confidence.<br>• Focus/internal motivation.<br>• Know yourself/be yourself. |

Decreasing the need for vigilance freed up valuable mental bandwidth for these students so they had more left for learning. Like the students who listened to their fellow students' Life Reports, realizing what we have in common can reduce vigilance, increase a sense of belonging, and free up cognitive resources for learning and personal growth.

## "Unpacking Privilege"

Using Peggy McIntosh's (1988) concepts, students can be supported to talk about their positions of privilege or disadvantage and what that means for all of us. We can talk about privilege in a U.S. context or a global one, changing the sense of relative privilege and disadvantage for almost all of us. Understanding the ideas of privilege and lack of privilege can help students look differently at their life and the conditions that have brought them to the present. As with the Life Reports, students can see that many of us have followed divergent paths to get to this specific classroom and that we each bring with us different levels of skills, knowledge, and wisdom. We can begin to see that the tax on mental bandwidth varies with our life experiences and current situations and that we can support each other from our positions of strength or need.

I use the analogy of a baseball field (see Figure 12.1) to talk about privilege. I introduce the idea that a person in the United States who has inherited wealth and has done well in life can think that he hit a home run, not

**Figure 12.1.**  Privilege discussion: Baseball field.

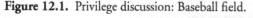
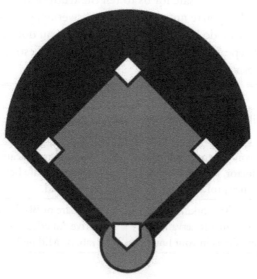

realizing that he was born on third base. I ask the students to explain where on the field they think they were born. We talk about why it's important to acknowledge that people are not all born to the same set of opportunities and that the relative amount of effort it takes to make it to home plate depends on where you started.

The website Organizing for Power, Organizing for Change (organizingforpower.org) has many resources for examining privilege, including articles and exercises (Fithian, n.d.). In one exercise called "Step Forward, Step Back," students start out together on a line. As the instructor reads statements, students step forward or back in response. Statements refer to conditions of life, such as "Step back if you are Black, Latina, Native American, Indian, Asian, Arab, or Middle Eastern descent" and "Step forward if your family owned its own home." The exercise is done in silence, and students are instructed that participation is voluntary and that they can choose not to respond to an item if they feel uncomfortable. The visual of the physical movement up or down an imaginary social ladder is very effective to show students that there are differences and that, in most classes, no one is alone in his or her situation or background. Table 12.2 is slightly revised from the original that I found on the website. Some people have students sign an informed consent, in which they tell the students that participation is completely voluntary and caution them that the experience could elicit strong emotions.

#### TABLE 12.2
#### Step Forward, Step Back activity

*Instructions read by instructors*: "Participation in this game is voluntary. I realize that it's not always safe for us to tell the truth or reveal who we are. If I ask a question that you're not comfortable answering, you can simply stand where you are. Please do this exercise in silence. If you don't hear a question, ask me and I'll repeat it. If you don't understand a question, either make a guess or don't respond to it."

| Step Forward | Step Back |
|---|---|
| 1. If your family owned its own home. | 1. If either of your parents did not graduate from college. |
| 2. If you or anyone in your immediate family is a doctor, lawyer, minister, teacher, or other professional. | 2. If you did not vacation outside your home state before you were 18 years old. |
| 3. If you grew up with working-class people who were maids, servants, gardeners, or babysitters in your house. | 3. If you are of Black, Latina/o, Native American, Indian, Asian, Arab, or Middle Eastern descent. |

*(Continues)*

TABLE 12.2 *(Continued)*

| Step Forward | Step Back |
|---|---|
| 4. If you studied the history and culture of your ethnic ancestors in elementary and secondary school. | 4. If you have ever been denied a job, paid less for comparable work, or passed over for promotion by a less qualified man because of your gender. |
| 5. If you have ever written a letter to influence the outcome of a political decision. | 5. If you are a survivor of incest, rape, or abuse. |
| 6. If you are a man. | 6. If you were raised by someone other than both of your biological parents. |
| 7. If, as a White person, you ever worked in a job where people of color held more menial jobs, were paid less, or were otherwise harassed or discriminated against. | 7. If anyone in your family has had a problem with drug or alcohol abuse. |
| 8. If your family had more than 50 books in the house when you were growing up. | 8. If you ever felt an opportunity or experience was closed to you because you didn't know how to speak, dress, or act. |
| 9. If your family told you that you could be or do anything that you choose. | 9. If you have ever been unable to attend an event or gathering because it was not accessible to people with your disability. |
| 10. If, as a child, you were taken to art galleries, museums, or plays by a parent or other relative. | 10. If you have ever felt judged or uncomfortable because of the size, height, or shape of your body. |
| 11. If you ever attended a private school or summer camp. | 11. If your family taught you that police were people to be feared. |
| 12. If you grew up expecting that your family would pay for your college. | 12. If your parents told you that you were beautiful or pretty and therefore what you thought or did wasn't important. |
| 13. If you believe that police would help you in an emergency. | 13. If, as a child, you were ever hungry or worried that there would not be enough food. |
| 14. If you ever inherited, or expect to inherit, money or property. | 14. If your family was ever forced to move because it could not afford to pay the bills. |

*(Continues)*

**TABLE 12.2** *(Continued)*

| Step Forward | Step Back |
|---|---|
| 15. If you or one or both of your parents are or were a member of a labor union. | 15. If you are gay, lesbian, bisexual, or transgender. |
| 16. If most of your friends are the same race as you. | 16. If you or any member of your family has been incarcerated for reasons other than political activism. |
| 17. If people with power in your community look like you. | 17. If you have ever lived somewhere that didn't feel safe. |
| 18. If people you see in the media, TV, newspapers, and magazines look like you. | 18. If you have ever hesitated to reveal your or your family's religious tradition. |
| 19. If most of your teachers in elementary school and high school looked like you. | 19. If you or any member of your immediate family has ever been on public assistance. |
| 20. Your first language was English. | 20. You have a visible or hidden physical disability or impairment. |

As I conclude this chapter, we should consider Steele's (1997) caution about "rendering onto the right students the right intervention" (p. 624). We can easily make mistakes based on assumptions. For instance, it's not safe to assume that all members of stereotyped groups are disidentified with their academic self. If we do that, we can communicate to the identified students that we see them as academically deficient. We might be focusing on reducing stereotype threat when what they need are the resources, skills, and confidence to identify with, for instance, a certain area of study. Steele also suggested that even when it seems that basic skills are not there, we may want to give it a go with the challenge instead of (or with) the remediation.

> Giving challenging work to students conveys respect for their potential and thus shows them that they are not regarded through the lens of an ability-demeaning stereotype. . . . All students can be given challenging work at a challenging, not overwhelming, pace, especially in the context of supportive adult–student relationships. In contrast, remedial work reinforces in these students the possibility that they are being viewed stereotypically. And this, by increasing stereotype threat in the domain, can undermine performance. (p. 625)

One of the most hopeful features of virtually all of the interventions that I have mentioned here is that they are fairly brief, one class period or shorter, and can be done for no or very low cost. In addition, although I have suggested the interventions as a way to help poor and nonmajority students succeed academically, these students are not singled out to recieve the intervention alone. Rather, the intervention is done with an entire class or other mixed group, with very positive results for some and no harm done to others. Many researchers (J. Aronson, Fried, & Good, 2001; G. L. Cohen, Garcia, Apfel, & Master, 2006; Sherman et al., 2013; Walton & Cohen, 2007; T. D. Wilson & Linville, 1985) have found that interventions that benefit nonmajority students as a group usually have a neutral effect on White students as a group.

In their manual on mind-set interventions, Snipes, Fancsali, and Stoker (2012) talked about the necessary contextual factors that encourage ownership of learning. Their statement seems appropriate to conclude this section on interventions:

> Caring, respectful relationships among adults and students; opportunities to experience autonomy, challenge, and contributing to the greater good; and the communication of high expectations and personal assurances that success is possible, coupled with strong feedback that helps students navigate a path to achieve it. (p. 1)

Because not all of us are necessarily skilled in creating positive learning environments, it is important to emphasize the need for effective professional development for faculty and other instructors and student affairs professionals who are interested in applying these interventions (Yeager & Walton, 2011).

# 13

# INSTITUTIONAL STRUCTURES AND PROCESSES

S tudent affairs professionals and classroom instructors can apply attitudes and strategies at an individual level to improve bandwidth, but the institution as a whole can address structural issues to maximize identity safety cues and minimize identity threat. Institutions can pay attention to and change things in the campus environment, as compared to internal psychological states or broad societal issues such as poverty and racism, that could significantly change the perception of the space in terms of identity safety. Such changes could ease students' worries that bad things might happen to them because of some aspect of their identity. Summarizing several studies about campus climate, Solórzano, Ceja, and Yosso (2000) concluded,

> When a collegiate racial climate is positive, it includes at least four elements: (a) the inclusion of students, faculty, and administrators of color; (b) a curriculum that reflects the historical and contemporary experiences of people of color; (c) programs to support the recruitment, retention, and graduation of students of color; and (d) a college/university mission that reinforces the institution's commitment to pluralism. (p. 62)

## Critical Mass

Students who are members of negatively stereotyped racial, socioeconomic, or ethnic groups perform less well in college, at least partially because of the pressure of identity threat. Identity threat results in a depletion of mental bandwidth that adds to the already significant disadvantages of being part of those groups. That means that even when Black and Latino students work hard to catch up to their White and Asian classmates, they still have to fight the effects of identity threat. Massey, Charles, Lundy, and Fischer (2002) conducted a series of interviews with nearly 4,000 White, Black, Asian, and Latino students who were admitted to selective colleges and universities in the United States. The interviews took place over the students' first three years of college. They found that even privileged students in these groups had an identity threat pressure working against their academic achievement. They did find one condition that alleviated the pressure: Black and Latino professors. Both Black and Latino students reported no stereotype threat in classes in which the professor was Black or Latino. Institutions could work intentionally to hire racial/ethnic nonmajority faculty at least in the same proportions as the student population, with a goal of creating a critical mass that would serve to support the retention of both the faculty and the students.

> The term "critical mass" refers to the point at which there are enough minorities in a setting, like a school or workplace, that individual minorities no longer feel uncomfortable there because they are minorities—in our terms, they no longer feel an interfering level of identity threat. (Steele, 2010, p. 135)

Dasgupta (2011) considered high-achieving women and minorities who, in spite of high performance, chose not to pursue academic or professional paths in high-achievement areas. He wondered if this disconnect was due to stereotype threat. He used what he called the "stereotype inoculation model" to determine what circumstances of a school or work context might encourage people to go for the study area or profession that is more consistent with their demonstrated abilities. He suggested that two factors contribute to stereotype inoculation: "exposure to ingroup experts and peers in high-achievement contexts" (p. 233). Such exposure, Dasgupta asserted, acts like a "social vaccine" against self-doubt, especially early on when students or professionals are getting their bearings in the new setting. His work supports student groups such as Women in STEM, led by women faculty in science, technology, engineering, and mathematics (STEM) disciplines. It also suggests the helpfulness of having women and people of color in leadership roles at a university and more faculty of color in classrooms, where students in those groups could find role models. Specifically, Dasgupta said,

> Exposure to ingroup experts will be most beneficial if perceivers feel a subjective sense of connection or identification with them because subjective identification makes the path from one's present self to a future

"possible self" seem more attainable given that one can imagine following
the trajectory of the ingroup member. (p. 233)

Along with having more faculty of color in the classroom, another strategy
for minimizing identity threat for students in stereotyped groups is to avoid
having only one group member in a class section. When, for instance, a Black
student is the only Black student in a class in which almost all of the students
are White, his vigilance is turned up and consistently uses valuable cognitive resources, a bandwidth tax that may dampen his academic performance.
Being the sole representative in the class emphasizes a student's marginality
with what Steele (2010) called the "critical mass cue" (p. 140). To nonmajority students who find themselves in a class without identity mates, there is the
possibility "that we might have trouble being accepted, that we might lack
associates who share our sensibilities, that we might lack status and influence in the setting" (Steele, 2010, p. 141). When this happens to first-year
students who are already feeling insecure and hesitant, this identity threat
cue may be enough to cause them to withdraw from the situation, physically
or mentally. If enrollment in first-year general education classes could be
managed so that nonmajority students had several identity mates in each of
their classes, this identity safe setting might make a significant difference to
their sense of belonging and to their academic success as mental bandwidth
is freed up to devote to learning.

In addition, institutions should be aware of other areas where critical
mass—or the lack of it—could be communicating identity threat to students
and potential students. For instance, the racial/ethnic identity of university
employees, from the people who are working on the grounds to support staff
in offices to the managers and leaders in academic and student affairs, speaks
to the culture of an institution. On some campuses, students could easily
note a pattern that people of color and women are in the manual labor and
service positions and that the people in the highest leadership positions, who
make the decisions and have the power, are almost exclusively or predominantly White and male. Although that employee profile might not be unusual, as it reflects the reality of employment patterns in the United States, it
likely will not contribute to the sense of identity safety for students of color.
In fact, it will have the exact opposite effect, showing students of color that
their "place" at the university is beneath White people.

## Images

The formal mission statements of many institutions include words such
as *diversity* and *inclusion* that imply that they value pluralism and equity,

but what do people see and feel when they walk onto campus? Institutions communicate who is valued by their choice of images. When a student, sometimes with parents or other family members or friends, walks onto a campus, what are the images telling her about the chances that she will fit, that she will belong? In public spaces, such as student unions, classroom buildings, residence halls, and performing spaces, students are looking for pictures of people like them; they're constantly assessing the environment for cues that indicate identity safety or identity threat. If students of color see only, or predominantly, White students represented on posters, pictures, and websites, the identity cue is that there is not necessarily a place for them at this school. On the other hand, if students of color are visible in the images, identity safe cues are likely to be perceived. In many institutions in the United States, the portrait hall of current and past college presidents is going to display a row of White men. That is historical fact, and although there is no need to apologize for this reality, we might need to work hard to balance it with contemporary images that communicate to women and students of color that they are welcome and valued and that they, too, can succeed.

## Financial Needs

For students coming to college from poor and near-poor families, finances are a constant pressure. Federal, state, and institutional programs provide grants and low-interest loans for tuition and fees, books, and other educational expenses. But according to the College Board (S. C. Carlson, 2016),

> The biggest barrier to poor students' enrolling or staying in college is not tuition and fees, but everything else: rent, food, child care, gas, phone bills. Living costs represent more than 70 percent of the total cost of attending a two-year college. (para. 6)

Carlson cited a 2014 Federal Reserve survey reporting that a fifth of adults in the United States had attended some college but didn't have a degree. "The two most common reasons cited, particularly among black, Hispanic, and female respondents, were family responsibilities and the need to work" (para. 16). Carlson mentioned several examples of institutions that are attempting to help students meet some of their basic needs. Food assistance through food pantries and farmers' markets is being provided by Oregon State University and Humboldt State University. The Houston Food Bank, with San Jacinto College and Lone Star College, is offering "Food Scholarships" to students. Tacoma Community College is working with the Tacoma Housing Authority to provide rental subsidies to students. Staff at Indiana University–Purdue

University Indianapolis (IUPUI) have noted that some students get into very difficult financial situations partially due to their lack of financial management skills. IUPUI has hired an unpaid part-time social work student intern to help connect students to public benefits and other support and a full-time financial coach to help students with financial aid questions and financial crises. Even though it may seem impossible for many institutions, themselves facing drastic cuts in funding, to think about investing even more money to help students, if these are the barriers, it may be the cost of academic success for many students. Collaboration with community agencies and resources, where they exist, is likely to be very important.

## Conversations and Action

Dovidio and Gaertner (2005), in their discussion of aversive racism, contended that "racism has mutated to partially hide itself from view" (p. 1). Recall our earlier attention to "aversive" or "modern" racism. This is not in-your-face racism but the subtle kind that slips out in the words and behavior of liberal, well-meaning people who have been raised in a racist culture but are committed to not being racist. We want our society to be egalitarian and fair, and we want everyone to feel comfortable and welcome. In our efforts to create this kind of environment, we can make ourselves blind to racism and avoid confronting it when it is surely there. Dovidio and Gaertner have some "simple (but not easy)" suggestions (para. 27). If a person of color brings up race as an issue, listen! Try to understand the person's perspective without getting defensive. Slow down and really listen without trying to explain away the problem. They cautioned, "It is almost never completely safe for a person of color to challenge a dominant perception. Listen deeply" (para. 27).

They suggested that at the institutional level we look beyond the diversity of skin color and look at the "issues of race and power." We need to examine who has the power within an institution.

> With power comes the ability to affect frames of reference, style, rules and priorities. With a shift in power, issues that were unseen by whites for years and obvious to people of color emerge quickly as actionable items. . . . We must stop thinking that someone else will intervene in the state of emergency posed by institutional racism and begin to address the appalling realities of its effect actively, head-on and in deeply committed cross-cultural partnerships. (Dovidio & Gaertner, 2005, para. 27)

Strayhorn (2012) in his work on college students' sense of belonging, added his voice to urge us to confront systems of power and privilege at our institutions. He pointed out that efforts to nurture students' sense of belonging may be within social contexts that are removed from the predominant campus culture, such as sororities or fraternities for students of color, summer bridge programs, and race/ethnicity-based student groups. Even when, or maybe especially when, these efforts are successful, they might go on while the "larger institutional culture is unchallenged and unchanged" (Johnson, 2013).

So, we must have conversations, and we must *do something*. We have to examine who is at the table and who decides who is at the table. That's the power part. A term that has caught on in recent years is *inclusion*—the idea that higher education should be open to everyone and that welcoming diverse people and ideas into the process is good for everyone. J. Carlson (2015–2016) challenged that idea in "Against Being Inclusive":

> Inclusion would seem initially to constitute an improvement over exclusion; however, it masks dominance—the power to grant or deny inclusion—and so is, in some ways, less honest than outright exclusion. (p. 58)

He described beautifully the possibilities of real conversations in which we all could be transformed (and our institutions potentially transformed in the process). He described students who bring their whole self to the learning environment and put their previous knowledge and assumptions at risk in open consideration of contrasting ideas. For our institutions, he asserted,

> Inclusion into the given is not enough. Our journey away from exclusion must move beyond inclusion and enact a more intrinsically pluralistic first principle for construing higher education itself—an epistemology of diversity that envelops and informs all we say and do, in an educational trajectory that has a radically open future. (p. 58)

Only when we can create institutional environments where all of our students come to the classroom with maximum mental bandwidth for learning will we begin to see the possibilities of a "radically open future."

# 14

# CASE STUDY

## Georgia State University

Georgia State University (GSU) has been the focus of national attention because of its astonishing success in increasing retention and graduation rates among its majority–minority student body. Since the establishment of the first Freshman Learning Communities (FLCs) in 2003, the institution has implemented over a dozen major "strategic programs" all focused on increasing the student success of its undergraduate population that is 63% non-White and 59% Pell eligible. See the *2015 Status Report: Georgia State University Complete College Georgia* (GSU, 2015) for a complete description of the initiative and the results.

Recently, with colleagues from my university, I spent a couple of days at GSU to learn about how the university accomplished this major turnaround in student outcomes. Throughout the visit, I felt that I was at a growth mindset institution, one where decisions were made based on evidence and where risks were taken with new programs that might or might not work. If they didn't work, they were discontinued, and if they did work, efforts were made to scale them up so that more students—in some cases, all students—had access to the potential positive outcomes. GSU stated

> The most distinctive *principle* guiding our efforts has been a pledge to improve student outcomes through *inclusion* rather than *exclusion*. We committed ourselves to not improve our graduation rates by turning our backs on the low-income, underrepresented and first-generation students that we have traditionally served. To the contrary: we pledged to increase the number of underrepresented, first-generation and Pell students enrolled and to serve them better. We committed to achieving improved outcomes for our students not merely at Georgia State University but in their lives and careers after graduation. (GSU, 2015, p. 8)

Even though no one at GSU specifically referred to students' mental bandwidth, it seems to me that their great success can be attributed to the initiatives and interventions they have put in place since 2003, which have functioned to free up the bandwidth of their students so they could focus on academics. When students are economically insecure and their nonmajority status comes with constant identity threat situations, one relatively minor stumble often derails them so much that they stop out of college, and many never return. I will briefly describe several of the approaches taken by GSU that, together, have resulted in significant increases in student outcomes, measured primarily by retention and graduation rates. In 2003, GSU's graduation rate for White students was 32%, for Black students 29% (18% for Black males), and for Latino students 22%. Graduation rates for Pell-eligible students were far below those of non-Pell students. In 2015, those achievement gaps were gone. The total graduation rate had improved by 22 percentage points, up 19 points for White students, 28 points for Black students, and 32 points for Latino students. Pell-eligible students' graduation rates over the past three years, on average, were equal to the rates for all students. In 2015, the overall Pell graduation rate of 55% was higher by 2 percentage points than the non-Pell rate. During these years, GSU recruited more Pell-eligible and nonmajority students as well; between 2008 and 2015, the proportion of the undergraduate population who were Pell eligible increased from 32% to 59%, and the proportion of underrepresented minority students increased from 53% to 63%.

## Learning Communities, Meta-Majors, and Block Scheduling

Beginning in 2003, with an overall undergraduate graduation rate of just 32%, GSU started FLCs for some groups of freshmen. In its current form, the FLC program is an opt-out model; 95% of nonhonors freshmen participated in 2015 (up from 80% when it was an opt-in model beginning in 2013). In 2012, GSU established meta-majors, which are academic disciplinary clusters: STEM, arts and humanities, health sciences, natural sciences, education, policy and social science, business, and exploratory. Each non-honors freshman signs up for one of the meta-majors and then chooses from a long list of block schedules—"pre-populated course timetables including courses relevant to their first year of study" (GSU, 2015, p. 16). From these selections, groups of 25 students are formed into FLCs, sharing five or six courses in addition to the one-credit-hour orientation to college course. The block schedules are intentionally designed so that students have time to work and/or can plan for child care. For instance, a block schedule might have all classes between 8:00 a.m. and 12:00 p.m. on Tuesday and Thursday or classes only in the afternoons on Monday and Wednesday.

How do meta-majors, FLCs, and block schedules free up bandwidth? Many freshmen are not certain about what they want to study and what specific job they want to have after graduation. In fact, many first-generation students may have heard of only a small fraction of the possibilities for majors. Many freshmen, however, have some ideas about the kinds of things that interest them. With meta-majors, students can choose an area of study, and their schedule is constructed so that every course is guaranteed to apply to any major within that meta-major. This means that students don't need to spend precious bandwidth worrying about taking the wrong classes that might not "count" later when they decide on a major. The block scheduling frees up bandwidth that they would otherwise use in trying to piece together a schedule from a list of hundreds of available courses. They can take this predetermined schedule and work out with an employer or a child care provider when they will be in class within specific blocks of time.

The FLCs contribute significantly to students' sense of both belonging and mattering. Every student will have ample opportunity to get to know 24 other students in the orientation class and in at least one other class, such as English composition or public speaking, in which only the 25 of them will be enrolled. In addition, students will have four other classes in which they will be with these 24 students, as well as with sophomore, junior, and senior students, so there are more chances to get connected and to learn from students who have been around the university for a year or more. With the connection to this small group of students, it is more likely that students will have a sense that they are a significant part of GSU and that someone will notice if they don't come to class. In turn, each student will matter to some other students, as it is common for small study and social groups to form out of the FLC.

## Academic Advising and Analytics

Another important connecting point in the first year is the academic adviser. GSU has invested significantly in increasing its advising staff; each adviser has about 300 students for whom she or he is responsible. This very reasonable ratio combines with powerful analytics to create an advising system that is responsive practically to the minute, intervening with students before they get derailed. Looking at historical data on student enrollments, grades, persistence, graduation, financial aid, and other data, GSU identified over 800 incidents that now trigger an alert to students and advisers, so that immediate intervention can happen. For instance, if a student enrolls in the wrong class for her major (e.g., a prenursing student signs up for a general anatomy and physiology class instead of the preprofessional section, or a social sciences major fails to enroll in a prerequisite class, without which he will be delayed a full semester) an alert is triggered. Each morning, advisers look at their list of students, beginning with the ones for whom there is a "high-risk" designation, and get to work to try to resolve the current or potential missteps that might temporarily or permanently derail a student.

The positive effect on bandwidth of trusting that someone is watching out for you and that you will get a notice if you are about to head down a side path is incalculable. Many first-generation, nonmajority, and economically insecure students feel like they're in over their heads at college, with belongingness uncertainty, identity threat, and money worries dogging them at every step. The last thing they need is to add the nagging worry that they may be wasting their time and money on the wrong class. At GSU's advising center, there are 70 advisers who deal mostly with students in their first three years (advisers within the colleges pick students up as they get within a year or so of graduation). Students enter an environment that is invitational. The center has an open floor plan with comfortable spaces to hang out and people to greet them who are knowledgeable and whose job it is to guide students to help. It feels like an identity safe place, with professional staff whose race and ethnicity match that of the students (advising staff are 70% non-White compared to 63% of students) (T. Renick, personal communication, August 10, 2016). The center is service focused; each day, there are two advisers who have no scheduled appointments so that walk-in students can be seen in a timely manner. Student advising records are housed on a common system, so that any adviser can bring up a student's record and can see the specific situation, which is updated nightly. Many students get the help they need in the walk-in visit, and others leave with a future appointment set with their own adviser.

## Instruction

In 2004, GSU began to build its supplemental instruction program. For the fall of 2016, there were students enlisted as class supplemental instructors (SIs) in over 1,000 sections. Many of these students, who were recruited to be peer tutors from those who did very well in a class, were already working on campus in some capacity, so those funds could be shifted to pay them for being a class SI (a function likely to be much more central to student success than working in an office or answering a bank of telephones). Many of the students were also eligible for federal work-study, which increased the affordability of the program for the university. Almost 10,000 students were in classes with SIs during the 2013–2014 academic year. Institutional research showed that students who went to at least five supplemental instruction sessions during the semester showed a mean GPA increase of half a letter grade. The SI program provides belonging and self-efficacy benefits for the SIs and academic support for the students who use the instruction, resulting in potential bandwidth recovery for everyone involved.

## Financial Help

For the majority of students who attend GSU, finances are a serious challenge. Institutional research revealed the reality of how many students had stopped out, temporarily or permanently, because of the lack of sometimes only small amounts of money. GSU has used funds strategically to keep students on track with their Panther Retention Grant program, which is available to students who have unmet financial need, are on track to graduate, and have a modest balance in their account that is keeping them from enrolling in classes. In these conditions, students are awarded a microgrant; nearly 2,000 grants were awarded in 2013–2014. Among seniors who received the grant, 61% graduated within two semesters of receipt, and another 21% were still enrolled one year after receiving the grant. Of freshmen who received the grant in fall 2013, 93% returned in spring 2014, and 83% of these returned in fall 2014. "Many students lack the financial literacy to ensure that an otherwise sustainable amount of financial support is managed effectively through to the end of their degree" (GSU, 2015, p. 14). By providing these small grants to students who have run out of financial aid money, GSU is getting students through to graduation who might not otherwise make it. In addition, the institution has made a commitment to creating a dedicated financial counseling center, with the goal that far fewer students will experience financial shortfalls at the end of their degree. There is another financial support program, called Keep Hope Alive, that awards students $500 per semester after they lost the state-sponsored Hope Scholarship (which requires a certain minimum GPA) to encourage them to stay, recover, and get the state scholarship back.

There is a program called Success Academy, through which a group of freshmen who appear to be the most at risk according to a freshmen index come to GSU for a seven-week session in the summer before the fall semester starts. They take seven credit hours, including the one-hour orientation class. For students in preprofessional programs, GSU has identified several related health professions that require the same prerequisite and core courses and into which students can smoothly transition when, like 80% of prenursing majors, for example, they don't make it into the nursing program. Academic advisers, during the fall semester, come to each section of the orientation class to give a group advising talk and then present each student with a suggested schedule for the spring semester that an adviser has worked out based on the student's meta-major or major if he or she has declared one by that time. All of these programs have provided ready assistance and continual support to students, the majority of whom are likely operating with limited bandwidth because of poverty or racism or because of some other aspect of differentness that results in their experience of sociopsychological underminers.

The leaders at GSU made a decision several years ago that they were committed to serving the students in Atlanta and in the state of Georgia and to improving student outcomes. They did that not by getting different students but by removing institutional barriers—threats to mental bandwidth—to student success. As stated in the *Status Report,* "Our efforts over the past few years show that dramatic gains are indeed possible—not through changing the nature of the students served but through changing the nature of the institution that serves them" (GSU, 2015, p. 19). As part of their growth mind-set, GSU leadership and staff have made a commitment to share what they have done with other institutions. For the past two years, they have hosted teams from approximately 80 colleges and universities, and members of their leadership team routinely give talks and conduct workshops across the United States. We found enthusiastic allies at GSU, people committed to student success who seem to have created a caring culture that is producing great benefits for their students. In my view, the differential effect of this set of interventions on White, economically secure students compared with non-White, Pell-eligible students is evidence that there is more at play here than simply the need for more money, academic support, or guidance. The differential results suggest that the negative effects of poverty and racism deplete students' mental bandwidth and that these interventions, singly and as a group, helped these specific students recover enough bandwidth to change outcomes significantly.

# CONCLUSION

A sense of belonging seems to be fundamental, an essential element of the learning environment upon which all others are predicated. We need to make sure the messages on our campuses and learning environments that communicate "identity threat" are outweighed by "identity safety" cues (Steele, 2010), creating what we might call a macro "counter-space" (Steele, 2010) in which students' stress responses can be quieted. These are spaces in which students can feel that they are among friends and supporters and where they can ask for and receive help when they need it. We must transform our institutions so that the entire enterprise operates from a growth mind-set (Dweck, 2006), where mistakes and missteps are seen as excellent opportunities to develop our individual and collective brain. We must draw out, acknowledge, and value the funds of knowledge that each of our students brings to the learning environment. We must have authentic conversations about race and social class and other societal dynamics that divide us and figure out ways to live together that uplift instead of undermine.

In a world in which there are serious problems to solve, we can no longer afford to have more than half of our population undereducated and underskilled because their mental bandwidth is being consumed by poverty, racism, and other differentisms. Maybe someday all students will arrive at college with their full mental bandwidths intact, but until then, it is our responsibility to help them regain their lost cognitive resources so they can learn and grow and, as adults, live a meaningful life and contribute positively to the future of our society and the world.

# REFERENCES

Adds, P., Hall, M., Higgins, R., & Higgins, T. R. (2011, October). Ask the posts of our house: Using cultural spaces to encourage quality learning in higher education. *Teaching in Higher Education, 16*(5), 541–551.

Alexander, D. (2013, December 13). Racism literally costs Americans $2 trillion . . . . Ready to stop payment? *TakePart*. Retrieved from http://www.takepart. com/article/2013/12/13/racism-literally-costs-america-too-much-continue

Alexander, M. (2012). *The new Jim Crow: Mass incarceration in the age of colorblindness*. New York, NY: New Press.

American College Health Association–National College Health Assessment. (2015, Spring). *Spring 2015 reference group executive summary*. Hanover, MD: American College Health Association.

American Public Health Association. (2015, March). *Better health through equity: Case studies in reframing public health work*. Washington, DC: Author.

Andre Gide quotes. (n.d.). Retrieved from http://www.goodreads.com/quotes/4661-man-cannot-discover-new-oceans-unless-he-has-the-courage

Aronson, J., Fried, C. B., & Good, C. (2001). Reducing the effects of stereotype threat on African American college students by shaping theories of intelligence. *Journal of Experimental Social Psychology, 38*, 113–125.

Aronson, J., Lustina, M. J., Good, C., Keough, K., Steele, C. M., & Brown, J. (1998). When White men can't do math: Necessary and sufficient factors in stereotype threat. *Journal of Experimental Social Psychology, 35*(1), 29–46.

Association for Psychological Science. (2007, September 24). Racism's cognitive toll: Subtle discrimination is more taxing on the brain. *Science Daily*. Retrieved from https://www.sciencedaily.com/releases/2007/09/070919093316.htm

Association of American Colleges & Universities. (2015). Step up and lead for equity: What higher education can do to reverse our deepening divides. Retrieved from www.aacu.org/diversity/publications

Bachman, J. G., O'Malley, P. M., Freedman-Doan, P., Trzesniewski, K. H., & Dennellan, M. B. (2011). Adolescent self-esteem: Differences by race/ethnicity, gender, and age. *Self Identity, 10*(4), 445–473.

Baggini, J. (2005, May 12). Wisdom's folly. *The Guardian*. Retrieved from https://www.theguardian.com/theguardian/2005/may/12/features11.g24

Bandura, A., & Schunk, D. H. (1981). Cultivating competence, self-efficacy, and intrinsic interest through proximal self-motivation. *Journal of Personality and Social Psychology, 41*, 586–598.

Barnes, G. L. (2008). Perspectives of African-American women on infant mortality. *Social Work Health Care, 47*(3), 293–305.

Barr, D. A. (2014). *Health disparities in the United States: Social class, race, ethnicity, and health.* Baltimore, MD: Johns Hopkins University Press.

Blackwell, L. S., Trzesniewski, K. H., & Dweck, C. S. (2007). Theories of intelligence predict achievement across an adolescent transition: A longitudinal study and an intervention. *Child Development, 78*(1), 246–263.

Blair, I., & Banaji, M. (1996). Automatic and controlled processes in stereotyping priming. *Journal of Personality and Social Psychology, 70,* 1142–1163.

Bligh, D. A. (1972). *What's the use of lectures?* Exeter, UK: Intellect.

Blow, F. C., Zeber, J. E., McCarthy, J. F., Valenstein, M., Gillon, L., & Bingham, C. R. (2004). Ethnicity and diagnostic patterns in veterans with psychoses. *Social Psychiatry and Psychiatric Epidemiology Journal, 39*(10), 841–851.

Boucher, E. (2016, August 22). It's time to ditch our deadlines. *The Chronicle of Higher Education.* Retrieved from http://www.chronicle.com/article/It-s-Time-to-Ditch-Our/237530

Braveman, P. (2008, December). *The unsolved mystery of racial disparities in birth outcomes: Is racism-related stress a missing part of the puzzle?* Presented at the National Institutes of Health Summit: The Science of Eliminating Health Disparities.

Bright, S. J. (2002). The social cognitive perception of why racism exists and persists. Edith Cowan University. Retrieved from http://www.geocities.ws/stephen_j_bright/studies/Racism.htm

Brown, B. (2014). 'You miss 100% of the shots you don't take.' You need to start shooting at your goals. *Forbes.* Retrieved from https://www.forbes.com/sites/actiontrumpseverything/2014/01/12/you-miss-100-of-the-shots-you-dont-take-so-start-shooting-at-your-goal/#bcbe11b6a40d

Brown, H. J. Jr (1991). *P.S. I love you.* Nashville, TN: Thomas Nelson.

Bump, N. (2016, February 12). Mattering: Why it matters for college students. Retrieved from http://motivislearning.com/2016/02/12/mattering-why-it-matters-for-college-students/

California Community Colleges Student Mental Health Program. (n.d.). *Supporting lesbian, gay, bisexual, and transgender students.* Student Mental Health Program Training and Technical Assistance for California Community Colleges. Retrieved from http://cccstudentmentalhealth.org/docs/SupportingLGBTQStudents.pdf

California Newsreel. (2008). *Unnatural causes . . . is inequality making us sick?* [Documentary series]. Retrieved from www.unnaturalcauses.org

Cardoza, K. (2016, January 20). First-generation college students are not succeeding in college, and money isn't the problem. *Washington Post.* Retrieved from https://www.washingtonpost.com/posteverything/wp/2016/01/20/first-generation-college-students-are-not-succeeding-in-college-and-money-isnt-the-problem/?utm_term=.bcbaf5caa6c8

Carlson, J. (2015, Fall–2016, Winter). Against being inclusive. *Liberal Education,* 58–63.

Carlson, S. C. (2016, March 6). On the path to graduation, life intervenes. *The Chronicle of Higher Education.* Retrieved from http://chronicle.com/article/On-the-Path-to-Graduation/235603

Carroll, G. (1998). Mundane extreme environmental stress and African American families: A case for recognizing different realities. *Journal of Comparative Family Studies, 29*(2), 271–284.

Carter, E. R., Peery, D., Richeson, J. A., & Murphy, M. C. (2015). Does cognitive depletion shape bias detection for minority group members? *Social Cognition, 33*(3), 241–254.

Casselman, B. (2014, April 30). Race gap narrows in college enrollment, but not in graduation. *FiveThirtyEight.* Retrieved from http://fivethirtyeight.com/features/race-gap-narrows-in-college-enrollment- but-not-in-graduation/

Centers for Disease Control and Prevention. (2014). LGBT youth. Retrieved from http://www.cdc.gov/lgbthealth/youth.htm

Centers for Disease Control and Prevention. (2015, November 13). Current cigarette smoking among adults: United States, 2005–2014. *Morbidity and Mortality Report, 64*(44),1233–1240.

Centers for Disease Control and Prevention. (n.d.). CDC report: Mental illness surveillance among adults in the United States. Retrieved from http://www.cdc .gov/mentalhealthsurveillance/fact_sheet.html

Centre for Confidence. (2008, 18 September). Carol Dweck Seminar: Creating Confident Individuals. Glasgow, Scotland.

Challis, J. R. (2004). Maternal corticotropin-releasing hormone, fetal growth, and preterm birth. *American Journal of Obstetrics and Gynecology, 191*(4), 1059–1060.

Chollar, R. (2013, June 17). 10 physical and emotional health concerns of LGBTQ students. Retrieved from https://www.campuspride.org/resources/10-physical-and-emotional-health-concerns-of-lgbt-students/

Christian, L. M., Glaser, R., Porter, K., & Iams, J. D. (2013). Stress-induced inflammatory responses in women: Effects of race and pregnancy. *Psychosomatic Medicine, 75*(7), 658–669.

Clark, K., & Quackenbush, M. (2014). *Transgender: Understanding gender differences* (brochure, Title No. 374). Scotts Valley, CA: ETR Associates.

Cohen, G. L., & Garcia, J. (2014). Educational theory, practice, and policy and the wisdom of social psychology. *Policy Insights From the Behavioral and Brain Sciences, 1*(1), 13–20.

Cohen, G. L., Garcia, J., Apful, N., & Master, A. (2006). Reducing the racial achievement gap: A social-psychological intervention. *Science, 313,* 1307–1310.

Cohen, G. L., Garcia, J., Purdie-Vaughns, V., Apfel, N., & Brzustoski, P. (2009). Recursive processes in self-affirmation: Intervening to close minority achievement gap. *Science, 324,* 400–403.

Cohen, G. L., Steele, C. M., & Ross, L. (1999, September). The mentor's dilemma: Providing critical feedback across the racial divide. *Personality and Social Psychology Bulletin, 25*(10), 1302–1318.

Cohen, S., Doyle, W. J., Skoner, D. P., Rabin, B. S., & Gwaltney, J. M. (1997). Social ties and susceptibility to the common cold. *Journal of the American Medical Association, 277*(24), 1940–1944.

Coker, T. R., Austin, S. B., & Schuster, M. A. (2010). The health and health care of lesbian, gay, and bisexual adolescents. *Annual Review of Public Health, 31*, 457–477.

Collins, J. W., David, R. J., Handler, A., Wall, S., & Andes, S. (2004). Very low birthweight in African American infants: The role of maternal exposure to interpersonal racial discrimination. *American Journal of Public Health, 94*(12), 2132–2138.

Costello, E. J., Compton, S. N., Keeler, G., & Angold, A. (2003). Relationships between poverty and psychopathology: A natural experiment. *Journal of the American Medical Association, 290*(15), 2023–2029.

Creswell, J. D., Welch, W. T., Taylor, S. E., Sherman, D. K., Gruenewald, T. L., & Mann, T. (2005). Affirmation of personal values buffers neuroendocrine and psychological stress responses. *American Psychological Association, 16*(11), 846–851.

Cullen, M. R., Cummins, C., & Fuchs, V. R. (2012). Geographic and racial variation in premature mortality in the U.S.: Analyzing the disparities. *PLOS One, 7*(4). Retrieved from http://journals.plos.org/plosone/article?id=10.1371/journal.pone.0032930

Da Costa Nunez, R. (2012, March 5). Homelessness: It's about race, not just poverty. *City Limits*. Retrieved from http://citylimits.org/2012/03/05/homelessness-its-about-race-not-just-poverty/

Dasgupta, N. (2011). Ingroup experts and peers as social vaccines who inoculate the self-concept: The stereotype inoculation model. *Psychological Inquiry, 22*, 231–246.

Day, L., Hanson, K., Maltby, J., Proctor, C., & Wood, A. (2010). Hope uniquely predicts objective academic achievement above intelligence, personality, and previous academic achievement. *Journal of Research in Personality, 44*, 550–553.

Debbink, M. P., & Bader, M. D. (2011). Racial residential segregation and low birth weight in Michigan's metropolitan areas. *American Journal of Public Health, 101*(9), 1714–1720.

DeNavas-Walt, C., & Proctor, B. D. (2015, September). *Income and poverty in the United States: 2014; Current population reports*. Washington, DC: U.S. Census Bureau, U.S. Department of Commerce. Retrieved from https://www.census.gov/content/dam/Census/library/publications/2015/demo/p60-252.pdf

Department of Health and Human Services. (n.d.). Executive summary: Mental health: Culture, race, and ethnicity. *Mental Health: A report of the surgeon general*. Retrieved from http://www.ct.gov/dmhas/lib/dmhas/publications/mhethnicity.pdf

De Weerth, C., & Buitelaar, J. K. (2005). Cortisol awakening response in pregnant women. *Psychoneuroendocrinology, 30*(9), 902–907.

Digest of Education Statistics. (2015a). Percentage of high school dropouts among persons 16 to 24 years old (status dropout rate), by sex and race/ethnicity: Selected years, 1960 through 2014. Retrieved from https://nces.ed.gov/programs/digest/d15/tables/dt15_219.70.asp

Digest of Education Statistics. (2015b). Percentage of persons 25 to 29 years old with selected levels of educational attainment, by race/ethnicity and sex: Selected years, 1920 through 2015. Retrieved from https://nces.ed.gov/programs/digest/d13/tables/dt13_104.20.asp

Do, D. P. (2009). The dynamics of income and neighborhood context for population health: Do long-term measures of socioeconomic status explain more of the Black/White health disparity than single-point-in-time measures? *Social Science and Medicine, 68*(8), 1368–1375.

Do not follow. (2014). Retrieved from http://quoteinvestigator.com/2014/06/19/new-path/

Dominguez, T. P. (2008). Race, racism, and racial disparities in adverse birth outcomes. *Clinical Obstetrics and Gynecology, 51*(2), 360–370.

Dominguez, T. P., Dunkel-Schetter, C., Glynn, L. M., Hobel, C., & Sandman, C. A. (2008). Racial differences in birth outcomes: The role of general, pregnancy, and racism stress. *Health Psychology, 27*(2), 194–203.

Dovidio, J. F., & Gaertner, S. L. (2005). Color blind or just plain blind? The pernicious nature of contemporary racism. *The NonProfit Quarterly, 12*(4).

Doyle, T., & Zakrajsek, T. (2013). *The new science of learning: How to learn in harmony with your brain.* Sterling, VA: Stylus.

Dweck, C. (2006). *Mindset: The new psychology of success.* New York, NY: Ballantine Books.

Dweck, C. (2014, November). The power of believing that you can improve. TEDXNorrkoping. Retrieved from https://www.ted.com/talks/carol_dweck_the_power_of_believing_that_you_ca n_improve

Do not follow. (2014). Retrieved from http://quoteinvestigator.com/2014/06/19/new-path/

Eleanor Roosevelt quotes. (n.d.). Retrieved from http://www.goodreads.com/quotes/25106-do-one-thing-every-day-that-scares-you

Ellis, J. R., & Gershenson, S. (2016, June 17). Peer advisors provide low-cost support for male undergraduates. *The Brown Center Chalkboard.* Retrieved from https://www.brookings.edu/blog/brown-center-chalkboard/2016/06/17/peer-advisors-provide-low-cost-support-for-male-undergraduates/

Emanuel, G. (2016, May 18). How to fix a graduation rate of 1 in 10? Ask the dropouts. *NPR Ed How Learning Happens.* Retrieved from http://www.npr.org/sections/ed/2016/05/28/479208574/how-to-fix-a-graduation-rate-of-1-in-10-ask-the- dropouts?utm_medium=RSS&utm_campaign=education

Entin, E. (2011, October 26). Poverty and mental health: Can the 2-way connection be broken? *The Atlantic.* Retrieved from https://www.theatlantic.com/health/archive/2011/10/poverty-and-mental-health-can-the-2-way-connection-be-broken/247275/

Ertel, K. A., James-Todd, T., Kleinman, K., Krieger, N., Gillman, M., Wright, R., & Rich-Edwards, J. (2012). Racial discrimination, response to unfair treatment, and depressive symptoms among pregnant Black and African American women in the United States. *Annals of Epidemiology, 22*(12), 840–846.

Executive Office of the President. (2014, December). *2014 native youth report.* Washington, DC: The White House.

Farbota, K. (2016, January 19). Black crime rates: What happens when numbers aren't neutral. *The Huffington Post.* Retrieved from http://www.huffingtonpost.com/kim-farbota/black-crime-rates- your-st_b_8078586.html

Federal Bureau of Prisons. (2016, June 25). Inmate race. Retrieved from https://www.bop.gov/about/statistics/statistics_inmate_race.jsp

Fedewa, A. L., & Ahn, S. (2011). The effects of bullying and peer victimization on sexual minority and heterosexual youth: A quantitative meta-analysis of the literature. *Journal of GLBT Family Studies, 7*(4), 398–418.

Feidberg, C. (2015). The science of scarcity. *Harvard Magazine,* 38-43.

Feldman, D. B., & Dreher, D. E. (2012). Can hope be changed in 90 minutes? Testing the efficacy of a single-session goal-pursuit intervention for college students. *Journal of Happiness Studies, 13*(4), 745–759.

Fischer, K. (2016, January 17). Engine of inequality. *The Chronicle of Higher Education.* Retrieved from http://chronicle.com/article/Engine-of-Inequality/234952

Fithian, L. (n.d.). Anti-oppression resources and exercises. Organizing for Power, Organizing for Change. Retrieved from http://organizingforpower.org/anti-oppression-resources-exercises/

Florida Council for Community Mental Health. (2007). Mental illness and poverty: A fact sheet. Retrieved from http://www.fccmh.org/resources/docs/MentalIllnessandPovery.pdf

Frank Scully quotes. (n.d.). Retrieved from http://www.goodreads.com/quotes/31336-why-not-go-out-on-a-limb-isn-t-that-where

Freeman, S., Eddy, S. L., McDonough, M., Smith, M. K., Okoroafor, H. J., & Wenderoth, M. P. (2014). Active learning increases student performance in science, engineering, and mathematics. *Proceedings of the National Academy of Sciences, 11*(23), 8410–8415.

Freeman, T. M., Anderman, L. H., & Jensen, J. M. (2007). Sense of belonging in college freshmen at the classroom and campus levels. *Journal of Experimental Education, 75*(1), 203–220.

Georgia State University (GSU). (2015). *2015 status report: Georgia State University Complete College Georgia.* Atlanta, GA: Author. Retrieved from http://enrollment.gsu.edu/files/2015/08/Georgia-State-University-CCG-Report-2015.pdf

Geronimus, A. T., Hicken, M., Keene, D., & Bound, J. (2006). "Weathering" and age patterns of allostatic load scores among Blacks and Whites in the United States. *American Journal of Public Health, 96*(5), 826–833.

Gershenson, S. (2015, August 18). The alarming effect of racial mismatch on teacher expectations. *The Brown Center Chalkboard.* Retrieved from http://www.brookings.edu/blogs/brown-center-chalkboard/posts/2015/08/18-teacher-expectations-gershenson

Gilman, S. E., Kawachi, I., Fitzmaurice, G. M., & Buka, L. (2003). Socio-economic status, family disruption and residential stability in childhood: Relation to onset recurrence and remission of major depression. *Psychological Medicine, 33*, 1341–1355.

Giscombé, C. L., & Lobel, M. (2005). Explaining disproportionately high rates of adverse birth outcomes among African Americans: The impact of stress, racism, and related factors in pregnancy. *Psychological Bulletin, 131*(5), 662–683.

Glisczinski, D. J. (2011). Lighting up the mind: Transforming learning through the applied scholarship of cognitive neuroscience. *International Journal for the Scholarship of Teaching and Learning, 5*(1), 1–13.

Goff, P. A., Steele, C. M., & Davies, P. G. (2008). The space between us: Stereotype threat and distance in interracial contexts. *Journal of Personality and Social Psychology, 94*, 91–107.

Gonzales, N., Moll, L., & Amanti, C. (1995). Introduction: Theorizing practices. In N. Gonzales, L. Moll, & C. Amanti (Eds.), *Funds of knowledge: Theorizing practices in households, communities, and classrooms* (pp. 1–24). Mahwah, NJ: Lawrence Erlbaum.

Good, C., Aronson, J., & Inzlicht, M. (2003). Improving adolescents' standardized test performance: An intervention to reduce the effects of stereotype threat. *Applied Developmental Psychology, 24*, 645–662.

Goode, E. (2002, December 17). The heavy cost of chronic stress. *The New York Times.* Retrieved from http://www.nytimes.com/2002/12/17/science/the-heavy-cost-of-chronic-stress.html

Gose, B. (2014, October 27). Helping Black men succeed in college. *The Chronicle of Higher Education.* Retrieved from http://chronicle.com/article/Helping-Black-Men-Succeed-in/149585/

Grant, H., & Dweck, C. S. (2003). Clarifying achievement goals and their impact. *Journal of Personality and Social Psychology, 85*(3), 541–553.

Grant, J. M., Mottet, L. A., & Tanis, J. (2011). *Injustice at every turn: A report of the national transgender discrimination survey.* Washington, DC: National Center for Transgender Equality and National Gay and Lesbian Task Force.

Grasgreen, A. (2012, July 6). Researchers apply hope theory to boost college student success. *Inside Higher Ed.* Retrieved from https://www.insidehighered.com/news/2012/07/06/researchers- apply-hope-theory-boost-college-student-success

Green, A. (2016, January 21). The cost of balancing academia and racism. *The Atlantic.* Retrieved from https://www.theatlantic.com/education/archive/2016/01/balancing-academia-racism/424887/

Hamblin, J. (2015). The paradox of effort: A medical case against too much self-control. *The Atlantic.* Retrieved from http://www.theatlantic.com/health/archive/2015/07/the-health-cost-of-upward-mobility/398486/

Harper, S. R. (2012a). *Black male student success in higher education: A report from the National Black Male College Achievement Study.* Philadelphia, PA: University of Pennsylvania Center for the Study of Race and Equity in Education. Retrieved from https://www.gse.upenn.edu/equity/sites/gse.upenn.edu.equity/files/publications/bmss.pdf

Harper, S. R., & Kuykendall, J. A. (2012). Institutional efforts to improve Black male student achievement: A standards-based approach. *Change, 44*(2), 23–29.

Harvard Kennedy School. (n.d.). About social capital. Retrieved from https://www .hks.harvard.edu/programs/saguaro/about-social-capital

Harvard School of Public Health. (2012, Fall). Public health and the U.S. economy. Retrieved from http://www.hsph.harvard.edu/news/magazine/public-health-economy-election/

Hayanga, A. J., Zeliadt, S. B., & Backhus, L. M. (2011). Residential segregation and lung cancer mortality in the United States. *Journal of the American College of Surgeons, 213*(3), S117.

Healthy People 2020. (2014). Lesbian, gay, bisexual, and transgender health. Retrieved from https://www.healthypeople.gov/2020/topics-objectives/topic/ lesbian-gay-bisexual-and-transgender-health

Hoffman, M., Richmond, J., Morrow, J., & Salomone, K. (2002). Investigating "sense of belonging" in first-year college students. *Journal of College Student Retention, 4*(3), 227–256.

Hulleman, C. S., & Harackiewicz, J. M. (2009). Promoting interest and performance in high school science classes. *Science, 326*, 1410–1412.

Human Rights Campaign (n.d.). *Glossary of terms.* Retrieved February 11, 2019 from https://www.hrc.org/resources/glossary-of-terms

Human Rights Campaign. (2012). Growing up LGBT in America. Retrieved from http://hrc-assets.s3-website-us-east-1.amazonaws.com//files/assets/resources/ Growing-Up-LGBT-in-America_Report.pdf

Irby, S. (2015, December 14). Black girls don't get to be depressed. *Cosmopolitan.* Retrieved from http://www.cosmopolitan.com/lifestyle/news/a50692/black-girls-dont-get-to-be-depressed/

James, S. A. (1994). John Henryism and the health of African-Americans. *Culture, Medicine and Psychiatry, 18*, 163–182.

Jaschik, S. (2014, October 27). Rose-Hulman plans to add new psychological test to admissions process. *Inside Higher Ed.* Retrieved from https://www.insidehighered .com/news/2014/10/27/rose-hulman-plans-add-new-psychological-test-admissions-process

Jaschik, S. (2015, September 3). SAT scores drop and racial gaps remain large. Retrieved from https://www.insidehighered.com/news/2015/09/03/sat-scores-drop-and-racial-gaps-remain-large

Jencks, C., & Phillips, M. (1998, March 1). The Black–White test score gap: Why it persists and what can be done. *Brookings.* Retrieved from https://www.brookings .edu/articles/the-black-white-test-score-gap-why-it-persists-and-what-can-be-done/

Jiang, Y., Ekono, M., & Skinner, C. (2015). *Basic facts about low-income children: Children under 18 years, 2013.* New York, NY: National Center for Children in Poverty. Retrieved from http://www.nccp.org/publications/pub_1100.html

John Augustus Shedd. (2017). Retrieved from https://en.wikiquote.org/wiki/John_ Augustus_Shedd

Johnson, D. R. (2013). College student's sense of belonging: A key to educational success for all students by Terrell L. Strayhorn [Book review]. *Journal of College Student Development, 54*(6), 662–663.

Jones, C. (2015). Interview with Camara Jones [Video]. Retrieved from https://www.youtube.com/watch?v=3BB3TMWX2So

Ka'ai, T. (2008). The role of marae in tertiary education institutions. *Te Kaharoa, 1*, 193–202.

Karp, M. M., O'Gara, L., & Hughes, K. L. (2008). *Do support services at community colleges encourage success or reproduce disadvantage?* (Working Paper No. 10). Community College Research Center, Teachers College, Columbia University, New York, NY. Retrieved from http://ccrc.tc.columbia.edu/media/k2/attachments/support-services-reproduce-disadvantage.pdf

Klein Dytham architecture. (2003). Pecha Kucha. Retrieved from http://www.klein-dytham.com/pechakucha/

Koring, H. (2005). Peer advising: A win-win initiative. *Academic Advising Today, 28*(2). Retrieved from http://www.nacada.ksu.edu/Resources/Academic-Advising-Today/View-Articles/Peer-Advising-A-Win-Win-Initiative.aspx

Kuzawa, C. W., & Sweet, E. (2009). Epigenetics and the embodiment of race: Developmental origins of U.S. racial disparities in cardiovascular health. *American Journal of Human Biology, 21*(1), 2–15.

Lambert, C. (2012, March–April). Twilight of the lecture. *Harvard Magazine.* Retrieved from http://harvardmagazine.com/2012/03/twilight-of-the-lecture

LaSala, M. C., & Frierson, D. (2012). African American youth and their families: Redefining masculinity, coping with racism and homophobia. *Gay, Lesbian, Bisexual, Transgender Family Studies, 8*, 428–445.

LeClere, F. B., Rogers, R. G., & Peters, K. D. (1997). Ethnicity and mortality in the United States: Individual and community correlates. *Social Forces, 76*(1), 169–198.

Lee, S. (2016, November 21). April Greiman-If a design doesn't feel good in your heart, it does not matter what your brain says [blog post]. Retrieved from https://go.distance.ncsu.edu/gd203/?p=20372

Levy, D. J., Heissel, J. A., Richeson, J. A., & Adam, E. K. (2016). Psychological and biological responses to race-based social stress as pathways to disparities in educational outcomes. *American Psychologist, 71*(6), 455–473.

LGBTQIA Resource Center. (2016). *LGBTQIA Resource Center glossary.* Retrieved from http://lgbtqia.ucdavis.edu/educated/glossary.html

Loucks, E. B., Pilote, L., Lunch, J. W., Richard, H., Almeida, N. D., Benjamin, E. J., & Murabito, J. M. (2010). Life course socioeconomic position is associated with inflammatory markers: The Framingham Offspring Study. *Social Science and Medicine, 71*(1), 187–195.

Luczaj, S. (2008, February 7). The toll of subtle racism. Retrieved from http://counsellingresource.com/features/2008/02/07/racism-cognitive-effects/

Lukianoff, G., & Haidt, J. (2015, September). The coddling of the American mind. *The Atlantic.* Retrieved from http://counsellingresource.com/features/2008/02/07/racism-cognitive-effects/

Macrae, C., Milne, A., & Bodenhausen, G. (1994). Stereotypes as energy-saving devices: A look inside the cognitive toolbox. *Journal of Personality and Social Psychology, 66*, 37–47.

Makrigiannakis, A., Semmler, M., Briese, V., Eckerle, H., Minas, V., Mylonas, I., . . . & Jeschke, U. (2007). Maternal serum corticotropin-releasing hormone and ACTH levels as predictive markers of premature labor. *International Journal of Gynaecology and Obstetrics, 97*(2), 115–119.

Manderscheid, R. (2013). Breaking the chains of mental illness that bind those in poverty. *Behavioral Healthcare.* Retrieved from http://www.behavioral.net/blogs/ron-manderscheid/breaking-chains-mental-illness-bind-those-poverty

Marriott, L., & Sim, D. (2014, August). *Indicators of inequality for Māori and Pacifica people* (Working Papers in Public Finance). Wellington, New Zealand: Victoria Business School. Retrieved from http://www.victoria.ac.nz/sacl/centres-and-institutes/cpf/publications/pdfs/2015/WP09_2014_Indicators-of-Inequality.pdf

Martin, J. A., Hamilton, B. E., Osterman, M. J. K., Curtin, S. C., & Matthews, M. S. (2015). Births: Final data for 2013. *National Vital Statistics Report, 64*(1), 1–65.

Masci, D., & Lipka, M. (2015, December 21). Where Christian churches, other religions stand on gay marriage. Retrieved from http://www.pewresearch.org/fact-tank/2015/12/21/where-christian-churches-stand-on-gay-marriage/

Masi, R., & Cooper, J. L. (2006). *Children's mental health.* New York, NY: Columbia University, National Center for Children in Poverty. Retrieved from http://www.nccp.org/publications/pub_687.html

Maslow, A. H. (1943). A theory of human motivation. *Psychological Review, 50,* 370–396. Retrieved from http://www.researchhistory.org/2012/06/16/maslows-hierarchy-of-needs/

Massey, D. S., Charles, C. Z., Lundy, G., & Fischer, M. J. (2002). *The source of the river: The social origins of freshman at America's selective colleges and universities.* Princeton, NJ: Princeton University Press.

Matthews, T. J., MacDorman, M. F., & Thoma, M. E. (2015). Infant mortality statistics from the 2013 period linked birth/infant death data set. *National Vital Statistics Reports, 64*(9), 1–28.

McEwen, B. S. (2002). Protective and damaging effects of stress mediators: The good and bad sides of the response to stress [Suppl. 1]. *Metabolism, 51*(6), 2–4.

McGuire, T. G., & Miranda, J. (2008). New evidence regarding racial and ethnic disparities in mental health: Policy implications. *Health Affairs, 27*(2), 393–403.

McIntosh, P. (1988). *White privilege and male privilege: A personal account of coming to see correspondences through work in women's studies.* Retrieved from http://www.collegeart.org/pdf/diversity/white-privilege-and-male-privilege.pdf

McMahon, S., & Horning, J. (2013, Fall). *Living below the line: Economic insecurity and America's families.* Washington, DC: Wider Opportunities for Women. Retrieved from http://www.wowonline.org/wp-content/uploads/2013/09/Living-Below-the-Line-Economic-Insecurity-and-Americas-Families-Fall-2013.pdf

Medina, J. (2008). *Brain rules: 12 principles for surviving and thriving at work, home, and school.* Seattle, WA: Pear Press.

Miller, B. (2015, February 24). Researchers discuss how sense of belonging boosts student success rate. *UDaily.* Retrieved from http://www.udel.edu/udaily/2015/feb/student-success-022415.html

Miller, G. (2009). *Visible learning by John Hattie: Summary*. North Tyneside EAZ Consultant.

Miller, G. E., Yu, T., Chen, E., & Brody, G. H. (2015). Self-control forecasts better psychosocial outcomes but faster epigenetic aging in low-SES youth. *Proceedings of the National Academy of Sciences, 112*(33), 10325–10330.

Molnar, S. (2015). *Racial disparities in birth outcomes and racial discrimination as an independent risk factor affecting maternal, infant, and child health (Executive Summary)*. International Center for Traditional Childbearing, International Cesarean Awareness Network, Midwives Alliance of North America, and Elephant Circle.

Moore, T.-L. M. B., & Shaughnessy, M. F. (2012). Carol Dweck's views on achievement and intelligence: Implications for education. *Research Journal in Organizational Psychology and Educational Studies, 1*(3), 174–184.

Morisano, D., Hirsh, J. B., Peterson, J. B., Pihl, R. O., & Shore, B. M. (2010). Setting, elaborating, and reflecting on personal goals improves academic performance. *Journal of Applied Psychology, 95*(2), 255–264.

Mullainathan, S., & Shafir, E. (2013). *Scarcity: The new science of having less and how it defines our lives*. New York, NY: Picador/Henry Holt.

Narcisse, E. (2014, August 20). All this racism is exhausting. Retrieved from http://tmi.kotaku.com/all-this-racism-is-exhausting-1624560251

National Center for Education Statistics. (2015, May). Public high school graduation rates. Retrieved from http://nces.ed.gov/programs/coe/indicator_coi.asp

National Coalition for the Homeless. (2009, July). Minorities and homelessness. Retrieved from http://www.nationalhomeless.org/factsheets/minorities.html

National KIDS COUNT. (2015). Children in poverty by race and ethnicity. Retrieved from http://datacenter.kidscount.org/data/tables/44-children-in-poverty-by-race-and-ethnicity#detailed/1/any/false/869,36,868,867,133/10,11,9,12,1,185,13/324,323

Nuru-Jeter, A., Dominguez, T. P., Hammond, W. P., Leu, J., Skaff, M., Egerter, S., Jones, C. P., et al. (2009). "It's the skin you're in": African-American women talk about their experiences of racism; An exploratory study to develop measures of racism for birth outcome studies. *Maternal and Child Health Journal, 13*(1), 29–39.

O'Neal, C. (2014, July 28). Helping faculty free students from the misconceptions that chain them. Retrieved from https://prezi.com/9ttassggvorj/helping-faculty-free-students-from-the-misconceptions-that-chain-them/

Oyserman, D., Bybee, D., & Terry, K. (2006). Possible selves and academic outcomes: How and when possible selves impel action. *Journal of Personality and Social Psychology, 91*(1), 188–204.

Park, R. E. (1928). Human migration and the marginal man. *American Journal of Sociology, 33*(6), 881–893.

Pearson, A. R., Dovidio, J. F., & Gaertner, S. L. (2009). The nature of contemporary prejudice: Insights from aversive racism. *Social and Personality Psychology Compass, 3*(3), 314–338.

Pierce, C., Carew, J., Pierce-Gonzalez, D., & Wills, D. (1978). An experiment in racism: TV commercials. In C. Pierce (Ed.), *Television and education* (pp. 62–68). Beverly Hills, CA: Sage.

Powell, A. (2016, February 2). The costs of inequality: When a fair shake isn't fair enough. *U.S. News & World Report.* Retrieved from http://www.usnews.com/news/articles/2016-02-02/the-costs-of-inequality-when-a-fair-shake-isnt-fair-enough

Rand, K. L., Martin, A. D., & Shea, A. M. (2011). Hope, but not optimism, predicts academic performance of law students beyond previous academic achievement. *Journal of Research in Personality, 45*(6), 683–686.

Rich-Edwards, J. W., & Grizzard, T. A. (2005). Psychosocial stress and neuroendo-crine mechanisms in preterm delivery [Suppl.]. *American Journal of Obstetrics and Gynecology, 192*(5), S30–S35.

R. L. G. (2013, April 10). How Black to be? *The Economist.* Retrieved from http://www.economist.com/blogs/johnson/2013/04/code-switching

Rodriguez, R. (1982). *The achievement of desire.* New York, NY: Bantam Books.

Rosenberg, L., Palmer, J. R., Wise, L. A., Horton, N. J., & Corwin, M. J. (2002). Perceptions of racial discrimination and the risk of preterm birth. *Epidemiology, 13*(6), 646–652.

Rosenberg, M., & McCullough, B. C. (1981). Mattering: Inferred significance and mental health among adolescents. *Research in Community and Mental Health, 2,* 163–182.

Russell, S. T., Ryan, C., Toomey, R. B., Diaz, R. M., & Sanchez, J. (2011). Lesbian, gay, bisexual, and transgender adolescent school victimization: Implications for young adult health and adjustment. *Journal of School Health, 81*(5), 223–230.

Russell, S. T., & Toomey, R. B. (2012). Men's sexual orientation and suicide: Evidence for developmental risk. *Social Science and Medicine, 74*(4), 523–529.

Ryan, C., Huebner, D., Diaz, R. M., & Sanchez, J. (2009). Family rejection as a predictor of negative health outcomes in White and Latino lesbian, gay, and bisexual young adults. *Pediatrics, 123,* 346–352.

Rydell, R. J., Shiffrin, R. M., Boucher, K. L., Van Loo, K. V., & Rydell, M. T. (2010). Stereotype threat prevents perceptual learning. *Proceedings of the National Academy of Sciences, 107*(32), 14042–14047.

Sakala, L. (2014, May). United States incarceration rates by race/ethnicity, 2010. Retrieved from http://www.prisonpolicy.org/graphs/2010rates/US.html

Sandman, C. A., Glynn, L., Schetter, C. D., Wadhwa, P., Garite, T., Chicz-DeMet, A., & Hobel, C. (2006). Elevated maternal cortisol early in pregnancy predicts third trimester levels of placental corticotropin releasing hormone (CRH): Priming the placental clock. *Peptides, 27*(6), 1457–1463.

Schlossberg, N. K. (1989). Marginality and mattering: Key issues in building community. *New Directions for Student Services, 1989*(48), 5–10.

Schott Foundation for Public Education. (2010). *Yes we can: The Schott 50 state report on public education and Black males.* Cambridge, MA: Author.

Sherman, D. K., Bunyan, D. P., Creswell, J. D., & Jaremka, L. M. (2009). Psychological vulnerability and stress: The effects of self-affirmation on sympathetic nervous system responses to naturalistic stressors. *Health Psychology, 28*(5), 554–562.

Sherman, D. K., Hartson, K. A., Binning, K. R., Purdie-Vaughns, V., Garcia, J., Taborsky-Barba, S., . . . & Cohen, G. L. (2013). Deflecting the trajectory and changing the narrative: How self-affirmation affects academic performance and motivation under identity threat. *Journal of Personality and Social Psychology*, *104*(4), 591–618.

Smith, D. J., & Valentine, T. (2012). The use and perceived effectiveness of instructional practices in two-year technical colleges. *Journal on Excellence in College Teaching*, *23*(1), 133–161. Retrieved from http://www.facultyfocus .com/articles/teaching-and-learning/lecture-continues-dominant-instructional-strategy/

Smith, W. A., Yosso, T. J., & Solórzano, D. G. (2006). Challenging racial battle fatigue on historically White campuses: A critical race examination of race-related stress. In C. A. Stanley (Ed.), *Faculty of color: Teaching in predominantly White colleges and universities* (pp. 299–327). Boston, MA: Anker.

Snipes, J., Fancsali, C., & Stoker, G. (2012). *Student academic mindset interventions: A review of the current landscape.* San Francisco, CA: Stupski Foundation.

Snyder, C. R. (2006, January). Approaching hope. *SGI Quarterly.* Retrieved from http://www.sgiquarterly.org/feature2006Jan-2.html

Snyder, C. R., Harris, C., Anderson, J. R., Holleran, S. A., Irving, L. M., Sigmon, S. T., . . . Harney, P. (1991). The will and the ways: Development and validation of an individual-differences measure of hope. *Journal of Personality and Social Psychology*, *60*(4), 570–585.

Snyder, C. R., Shorey, H. S., Cheavens, J., Pulvers, K. M., Adams, V. H., & Wiklund, C. (2002). Hope and academic success in college. *Journal Educational Psychology*, *94*(4), 820–826.

Solórzano, D., Ceja, M., & Yosso, T. (2000). Critical race theory, racial microaggressions, and campus racial climate: The experiences of African American college students. *Journal of Negro Education*, *69*(1–2), 60–73.

Solórzano, D., & Villalpando, O. (1998). Critical race theory, marginality, and the experience of minority students in higher education. In C. Torres & T. Mitchell (Eds.), *Emerging issues in the sociology of education: Comparative perspectives* (pp. 211–224). Albany, NY: State University of New York Press.

Spade, D. (2011). Some very basic tips for making higher education accessible to trans students and rethinking the way we talk about gendered bodies. *Radical Teacher*, *92*, 57–62, 80.

Spencer, S., Steele, C. M., & Quinn, D. (1999). Under suspicion of inability: Stereotype threat and women's math performance. *Journal of Experimental Social Psychology*, *35*, 4–28.

Steele, C. M. (1997). A threat in the air: How stereotypes shape intellectual identity and performance. *American Psychologist*, *52*(6), 613–629.

Steele, C. M. (2010). *Whistling Vivaldi: How stereotypes affect us and what we can do.* New York, NY: W. W. Norton.

Steele, C. M., & Aronson, J. (1995). Stereotype threat and intellectual test performance of African Americans. *Journal of Personality and Social Psychology*, *69*, 797–811.

Stone, C., Trisi, D., Sherman, A., & Horton, E. (2016). A guide to statistics on historical trends in income inequality. Retrieved from http://www.cbpp.org/research/poverty-and-inequality/a-guide-to-statistics-on-historical-trends-in-income-inequality

Straumanis, J. (2012, July–September). What we're learning about learning (and what we need to forget). *Planning for Higher Education.* Retrieved from http://stratolab.com/wp-content/uploads/2015/11/PHEV40N4_Article_What-Were-Learning-About-Learning.pdf

Strayhorn, T. L. (2012). *College students' sense of belonging: A key to educational success for all students.* New York, NY: Routledge.

Subramanian, S. V., Chen, J. T., Rehkopf, D. H., Waterman, P. D., & Krieger, N. (2005). Racial disparities in context: A multilevel analysis of neighborhood variations in poverty and excess mortality among Black populations in Massachusetts. *American Journal of Public Health, 95*(2), 260–265.

Substance Abuse and Mental Health Services Administration. (2015). Racial-ethnic differences in mental health service use among adults. Retrieved from http://www.samhsa.gov/data/sites/default/files/MHServicesUseAmongAdults/MHServicesUseAmongAdults.pdf

Sue, D. W. (2014, October 22). Microaggressions in everyday life: Implications for higher education. [Lecture]. Retrieved from http://oied.ncsu.edu/faculty/derald-wing-sue/

Sue, D. W., Capodilupo, C. M., Torino, G. C., Bucceri, J. M., Holder, A. M. B., Nadal, K. L., & Esquilin, M. (2007). Racial microaggressions in everyday life: Implication for clinical practice. *American Psychologist, 62*(4), 271–286.

Sugarman, S. (2010). Seeing past the fences: Finding funds of knowledge for ethical teaching. *The New Educator, 6,* 96–117.

Tatum, B. D. (1997). *"Why are all the Black kids sitting together in the cafeteria?" and other conversations about race.* New York, NY: Basic Books.

The best Richard DeVos quotes. (n.d.). http://www.ranker.com/list/a-list-of-famous-richard-devos-quotes/reference

Thompson, A. (2014, December 4). Voices: The exhausting task of being Black in America. *USA Today.* Retrieved from http://www.usatoday.com/story/life/people/2014/12/04/the-exhausting-task-of-being-black-in-america/19894223/

Thompson, C. (2008). *Come on shore and we will kill and eat you all: An unlikely love story.* London, UK: Bloomsbury.

Tollenaar, M. S., Beijers, R., Jansen, J., Riksen-Walraven, J. M. A., & de Weerth, C. (2011). Maternal prenatal stress and cortisol reactivity to stressors in human infants. *Stress, 14*(1), 53–65.

Toomey, R. B., Ryan, C., Diaz, R., Card, N. A., & Russell, S. T. (2010). Gender nonconforming lesbian, gay, bisexual, and transgender youth: School victimization and young adult psychosocial adjustment. *Developmental Psychology, 46*(6), 1580–1589.

Tough, P. (2014, May 15). Who gets to graduate? *The New York Times Magazine.* Retrieved from http://www.nytimes.com/2014/05/18/magazine/who-gets-to-graduate.html

Townsley, M. (2014, November 11). What is the difference between standards-based grading (or reporting) and competency-based education? Retrieved from http://www.competencyworks.org/analysis/what-is-the-difference-between-standards-based-grading/

Transphobia. (n.d.). *English Oxford Living Dictionaries.* Retrieved from https://en.oxforddictionaries.com/definition/transphobia

Turner, A. (2013). The business case for racial equality. Retrieved from http://altarum.org/sites/default/files/uploaded-publication-files/The%20Business%20Case%20for%20Racial%20Equity%20FINAL.pdf

Turner, C., Khrais, R., Lloyd, T., Olgin, A., Isensee, L., Vevea, B., & Carsen, D. (2016, April 18). Why America's schools have a money problem. Retrieved from http://www.npr.org/2016/04/18/474256366/why-americas-schools-have-a-money-problem

University of Illinois at Chicago. (2007, July 31). Disparities in infant mortality not related to race, study finds. *ScienceDaily.* Retrieved from www.sciencedaily.com/releases/2007/07/070730173400.htm

Valencia, R., & Solórzano, D. (1997). Contemporary deficit thinking (The Stanford Series on Education and Public Policy). In R. Valencia (Ed.), *The evolution of deficit thinking in educational thought and practice* (pp. 160–210). New York, NY: Falmer Press.

Vedantam, S. (2005, June 28). Racial disparities found in pinpointing mental illness. *Washington Post.* Retrieved from http://www.washingtonpost.com/wp-dyn/content/article/2005/06/27/AR2005062701496.html

Wadhwa, P. D., Garite, T. J., Porto, M., Glynn, L., Chicz-Demet, A., Dunkel-Schetter, C., & Sandman, C. A. (2004). Placental corticotropin-releasing hormone (CRH), spontaneous preterm birth, and fetal growth restriction: A prospective investigation. *American Journal of Obstetrics and Gynecology, 191*(4), 1063–1069.

Walton, G. M., & Cohen, G. L. (2007). A question of belonging: Race, social fit, and achievement. *Journal of Personality and Social Psychology, 92,* 82–96.

Walton, G. M., & Cohen, G. L. (2011). A brief social-belonging intervention improves academic and health outcomes among minority students. *Science, 331*(6023), 1447–1451.

Watanabe, T., & Song, J. (2015, November 12). College students confront subtler forms of bias: Slights and snubs. *Los Angeles Times.* Retrieved from http://www.latimes.com/local/education/la-me-college-microaggression-20151112-story.html

Watson, J. R. (1988). Neurobics. Retrieved from http://www.jamesrobertwatson.com/neurobics.html

What I know for sure. (n.d.). Retrieved from https://www.goodreads.com/work/quotes/40859663-what-i-know-for-sure Retrieved from http://www.jbhe.com/features/49_college_admissions-test.html

Whitman, S., Orsi, J., & Hurlbert, M. (2012). The racial disparity in breast cancer mortality in the 25 largest cities in the United States. *Cancer Epidemiology, 36,* e147–e151.

The widening racial scoring gap on the SAT college admissions test. (2016, March 16). *The Journal of Blacks in Higher Education.*

Wilkinson, R. G. (1999). Health, hierarchy, and social anxiety. *Annuls of the New York Academy of Science, 896,* 48–63.

Williams, J. J. (2013). *Applying cognitive science to online learning.* Retrieved from http://dx.doi.org/10.2139/ssrn.2535549

Williams, J. J., Paunesku, D., Haley, B., & Sohl-Dickstein, J. (2013). *Measurably increasing motivation in MOOCs.* In Proceedings of the 1st Workshop on Massive Open Online Courses at the 16th Annual Conference on Artificial Intelligence in Education, Memphis, TN.

Wilson, T. D., & Linville, P. W. (1985). Improving the performance of college freshmen with attributional techniques. *Journal of Personality and Social Psychology, 49,* 287–293.

Wilson, V., & Bivens, J. (2014). Estimates of unemployment rates by race and ethnicity at the MSA level for the third quarter of 2014. Retrieved from http://www.epi.org/publication/fed-unemployment-race/

Wolfe, T. (1940). *You can't go home again.* New York, NY, and London, UK: Harper and Row.

World Health Organization. (2007). *Breaking the vicious cycle between mental ill-health and poverty* (Sheet 1). Geneva, Switzerland: Author. Retrieved from http://www.who.int/mental_health/policy/development/1_Breakingviciouscycle_Infosheet.pdf

Yeager, D. S., Purdie-Vaughns, V., Garcia, J., Apfel, N., Brzustoski, P., Master, A. . . . Cohen, G. L. (2014). Breaking the cycle of mistrust: Wise interventions to provide critical feedback across the racial divide. *Journal of Experimental Psychology: General, 143*(2), 804–824.

Yeager, D. S., & Walton, G. M. (2011). Social-psychological interventions in education: They're not magic. *Review of Educational Research, 81,* 266–301.

Zastrow, C. H., & Kirst-Ashman, K. K. (2013). *Understanding human behavior and the social environment* (9th ed.). Belmont, CA: Cengage Learning (Brooks/Cole).

Cia Verschelden has worked in higher education for 31 years. A residence hall director during her doctoral research, she has also served as a faculty member in social work, women's studies, American ethnic studies, and nonviolence studies. She is currently vice president of academic and student affairs at City College of Chicago - Malcolm X College. Previously, she was the executive director of institutional assessment at the University of Central Oklahoma, where she taught in the sociology department and first-year experience program. She has been active in faculty leadership and in academic administration for 15 years, serving at public institutions, both four-year and community colleges. In every position, the one constant in her work and life has been advocacy for social justice and equity. She has a BS in psychology from Kansas State University, an MSW from the University of Connecticut, and an EdD from Harvard University. She is the parent of two homemade daughters and two adopted sons.

Most of all, McGuire is a fun writer. Personal and plainspoken, her style makes the pages fly by. (Any worries that this book might drown the reader in jargon should be alleviated by the appearance of the words 'metacognition, schmetacognition.') I would recommend this book in particular to educators working with students from underserved communities, as giving students access to these techniques will help ensure their success far beyond the boundaries of a single classroom."—*Reflective Teaching*, *Wabash Center*

**Sty/us**

22883 Quicksilver Drive
Sterling, VA 20166-2102                    Subscribe to our e-mail alerts: www.Styluspub.com

## Also available from Stylus

**Critical Mentoring**
*A Practical Guide*
Torie Weiston-Serdan

Foreword by Bernadette Sánchez

At this juncture when the demographics of our schools and colleges are rapidly changing, critical mentoring provides mentors with a new and essential transformational practice that challenges deficit-based notions of protégés; questions their forced adaptation to dominant ideology; counters the marginalization and minoritization of young people of color; and endows them with voice, power and choice to achieve in society while validating their culture and values.

"*Critical Mentoring* is a savory blend of theories, thoughtful concepts, and evidence. Perhaps its practical utility is the book's most praiseworthy feature. Readers learn not only what this unique brand of mentoring is but also how to more effectively develop and support youth, particularly those who are often pushed to the margins."—*Shaun R. Harper, Professor and Executive Director, University of Pennsylvania Center for the Study of Race & Equity in Education*

"This is a brilliant book. It is also an extremely useful one. Torie Weiston-Serdan has accomplished the great achievement of writing something that is immediately accessible, deeply thoughtful and theoretically-engaged, and of practical use to all those engaged in youth mentoring. It is also beautifully written. *Critical Mentoring* has the potential to change the paradigms of practice in the field."—*Viv Ellis, School of Education, Communication and Society, King's College London.*

**Teach Students How to Learn**
*Strategies You Can Incorporate Into Any Course to Improve Student Metacognition, Study Skills, and Motivation*
Saundra Yancy McGuire
With Stephanie McGuire

Foreword by Thomas Angelo

"With this book McGuire gives teachers the tools they need to move their students past the high school model of retention until regurgitation, helping them instead to internalize a more nuanced, flexible understanding of learning. To convey this understanding, McGuire focuses on student mind-set, encouraging educators to bring in everything from neurobiological models to fellow student success stories in order to help learners see that they are not stuck being 'bad' at something—that change is not only possible, but already well within reach.

*(Continues on previous page)*

**Association of American Colleges and Universities**

## About AAC&U

AAC&U is the leading national association concerned with the quality, vitality, and public standing of undergraduate liberal education. Its members are committed to extending the advantages of a liberal education to all students, regardless of academic specialization or intended career. Founded in 1915, AAC&U now comprises nearly 1,400 member institutions—including accredited public and private colleges, community colleges, research universities, and comprehensive universities of every type and size.

AAC&U functions as a catalyst and facilitator, forging links among presidents, administrators, and faculty members who are engaged in institutional and curricular planning. Its mission is to reinforce the collective commitment to liberal education and inclusive excellence at both the national and local levels, and to help individual institutions keep the quality of student learning at the core of their work as they evolve to meet new economic and social challenges.

Information about AAC&U membership, programs, and publications can be found at www.aacu.org